'Here is a book that puts a friendly arm
Christians, guiding and spurring them (
new life that Jesus offers. Alive with m
testimonies, Ralph's material, drawn from .... many years of experience
in evangelism and leadership, is refreshingly relevant and will help build
good, lasting foundations into the lives of his readers.'
Andy Arscott, *Senior Pastor, Frontiers Church, Exeter*

'In the pensions industry Ralph is well-known and appreciated as a man
of diligence and integrity. His life of faith in Jesus Christ, lived out
mostly in a secular setting, makes Ralph the ideal person to have
written this lively and encouraging book. I am sure it will help new
believers off their starting blocks and re-energise some of us who have
run part of the race.'
James Churcher, *Pensions Manager, Telegraph Media Group*

'I recommend Ralph Turner's book to you. This has been written out
of a vast wealth of experience, and contains distilled wisdom, which
will help you on your journey and growth in God, and hopefully help
you to know what is top priority so you avoid the traps other fall into!'
Rev. Gordon Hickson, *Associate Minister, St Aldates Church, Oxford*

'Many times in our lives good intentions do not become reality as we
lose our focus. But this book shows you how to make practical life
choices that enable you to live this new God-life forever! An excellent
book for individual or group discussions, full of real stories and advice
to equip, train and reach the generations to live passionately for God.'
Rachel Hickson, *Heartcry for Change, author of* Supernatural
Communication *and* Supernatural Breakthrough

'Ralph Turner doesn't practise his faith hidden away in a closet but in
the senior realms of business for some of the largest corporations in the
world. I have great respect for him in that, unlike many of us, Ralph has
perfected the art of seamlessly integrating his working life and the life
of Christian faith. His intention is to encourage the new Christian
through some of the basic aspects of "a Christian life that works". In
this book, Ralph succeeds in conveying timeless truths in everyday

language, sprinkled liberally with experiences he has had himself during his life as a Christian and those of others.'
Tony Hodges, *Managing Director, AHC Ltd*

'Liberally sprinkled with helpful anecdotes and quotes, this readable book by Ralph Turner will assist those making the transition from self-life to God-life to familiarise themselves with the terrain and atmosphere of the kingdom of Heaven. A good next step in the pilgrimage beyond Alpha.'
John Houghton, *Catalyst Ministries*

'I have had the enriching experience of making Ralph's acquaintance a few years ago. He has a rich insight into real life and the real difference that Jesus Christ makes in people – and he has the experience to prove it! There is no doubt that this book is a roadmap and spiritual digest that will assist each reader to tap into the difference Jesus makes and the difference He wants to make through us all. I am convinced God will use this book in a powerful way.'
Francois van Niekerk, *Senior Pastor, Hatfield Christian Church (Pretoria, South Africa) and Leader of The Christian Network, also in South Africa*

'Ralph Turner has written a refreshingly clear help book for new believers, which is rooted in his real life experience of walking by faith in God, giving it a ring of authenticity.''
Ewen Robertson, *Principal, Bible College of Wales*

'Ralph – whom I know through his work on pensions – has written a radiant book. It radiates with love for life, but in particular with love for God. And it explains clearly how even the most unlikely of us can share the joy which radiates from Ralph's life.'
Rt Hon Stephen Timms MP, *Minister for Employment and Welfare Reform*

God-life

God-life

Following Jesus and Going Deeper

Ralph Turner

New Wine Press

New Wine Ministries
PO Box 17
Chichester
West Sussex
United Kingdom
PO19 2AW

Dedication

In Memory of Three Friends and Mentors:
Roger Flavell, Ian Wilkie
and Richard Bartrop

Contents

Acknowledgements

Thanks to Nathan Turner, Pauline Stevens and Linda Pettican for their time and patience in reading through the manuscript. It reads better as a result!

Thanks to Simon Deeks for the initial encouragement to start writing again. I appreciate the friendship.

Thanks to Dave and Karen and everyone at KingsGate, the best church in the world (I'm slightly biased . . .). It's a privilege to serve and work with you all.

And a big thank you to a wonderful family: Roh, Nathan, Elspeth and Rob, Lois and Josh.

Author's Note

This book has deliberately been written as a 'book to read' – you can simply read it chapter by chapter and apply the message to your own life as you go.

However, I know many will want to dig deeper, so at the end of each chapter I have included a comprehensive set of notes with Bible verses and occasional comments. These notes may also be useful to you as a leader of a small group, wanting to take a chapter at a time and apply it in a group meeting context.

Either way, I hope you enjoy it!

Ralph Turner
Peterborough, 2008

Foreword

As a local church we have had the thrill and privilege of seeing hundreds of people coming to faith in Christ. Increasingly people are from a totally un-churched background. The need to fulfil the Great Commission, to make disciples of Jesus Christ, is more urgent than ever; a task that requires a lot more than an initial call to follow Christ, but an ongoing commitment to live for Christ. Many books and courses today are devoted to such a task.

One of the most successful courses over recent years has undoubtedly been Alpha. This continues to be one of the primary 'gateways' that we have seen here in Peterborough, both to help people come to faith, and to take their first few steps in the journey of faith. However, I will never forget the time when we as leaders here did a survey in the late 1990s of those who had started on Alpha, in comparison to those who had actually continued in their walk and were thoroughly established in the church. The findings were not encouraging. As one of my fellow leaders put it, we had a crack in the paving slabs and many people were falling through. So, under the deep conviction of the Lord, we repented as leaders for any lack on our part in caring for and discipling our new converts, and prayed for wisdom and a new anointing to keep those we had reached. Then we took a serious look at our then small group structure, and started making changes so that the gap between Alpha tables and regular small groups was much easier. Finally, we implemented a new Beta course (which we have just again revised in 2008), to try and smooth the transition from Alpha into healthy church life and results have been very encouraging. While some still struggle to keep going, the majority of those who come are not only staying, but growing, becoming relationally integrated and themselves becoming equipped to help fulfil God's purpose on the earth.

And so to this present work. Its author, Ralph Turner, is what Bill Hybels calls a 'high capacity volunteer' – someone who has been successful in the marketplace but consistently maintains a passion to serve God's Kingdom through the local church. This book flows out of that passion, with particular emphasis on seeing new Christians become grounded and grow healthily in their faith in Christ. It seeks to address some of the key issues that young believers face, such as what salvation is, our freedom in Christ and the place of prayer. Through a combination of doctrinal teaching, practical instruction and personal testimony, it aims to help the new believer in their walk with God. I pray that the lives of many will be transformed as a result of reading and applying the lessons of this book!

Dr David Smith
Senior Leader
KingsGate Community Church
Peterborough

Introduction

I had no idea how my life would change that night. Having heard someone explain the gospel for the first time, it made sense and I wanted to respond. So, late that night, on my own, I prayed a simple prayer. 'Lord God, if You are there, I want You to change my life.' That was it really. No lightning bolts. No funny feelings. Just a prayer.

I woke up the next day, feeling much the same. But I wasn't the same. Eternity had broken in to my fifteen-year-old life, and it was the start of an adventure that changed – and continues to change – my life.

For those of us who have prayed a prayer like that, for those of us who know God has begun something good in us, this book is written. Eternity has broken into our lives, we have God-life, and we will never be the same again.

The Cry of Another Country

I could feel the tension as the film reached its climax. It looked for a moment like the brilliant teacher, played by Robin Williams, would simply have to walk away. And then it happened. The boy stood on the desk. 'Captain, my captain,' he cried. Others followed. Soon nearly everyone was standing on their desks. The headmaster didn't know what to do. But for the audience – well, for me anyway! – it was a glorious moment. Hope had triumphed. The boys of *Dead Poets Society* (for that was the film) had shown that there really was more to life than conforming to the world they lived in. They were crying out for the 'more' that life offered.

The cry is in all of us. Whoever we are, whatever our background, we know that there must be more to life. The Bible says God has put eternity into the hearts of men.[1] It's there. It's in us. From our first awakenings to life, we sense there must be more. But what do we do with that awareness? For many of us, by the time we reach our teenage years, the cry of eternity is hidden under layers of 'life'. Things around us have become more important. We are driven by adolescent needs – the need to conform, the need to rebel, the need to look like we are rebelling!

And we've made a good job of it, haven't we? Rebelling, I mean. Adam and Eve set the example and we have successfully followed in their footsteps. A rebellious people, cut off from the creator God, but still with that cry within.

Then, for many of us, the day came. The day we reconnected with our God. The day we prayed a prayer and asked Jesus Christ to change our lives. In a real sense, eternity broke into our lives that day. We realised rebellion doesn't work. We realised that for us to know God, to know why we are here, to know our real purpose – that was what we were made for.

That's my story as a fifteen-year-old. If you've read this far, I expect it's your story too. At some time in your life, God broke in. God-life began. And you will never be the same again. For the rest of your life, you will belong to another country. And that cry within you will grow louder still, above and beyond the daily sirens of life.

What really happened that night

What really happened that night so long ago (yes, admission time – I'm a bit older than fifteen now!) when I prayed that prayer, asking God to forgive me and Jesus to come in to my life?

Paul the apostle sums it up well when he writes to the early Church. This is what he says:

> 'In [Christ] we have redemption through his blood, the forgiveness of sins, in accordance with the riches of God's grace that he lavished on us.'[2]

Redemption, forgiveness and grace. Strange Bible words. What is Paul talking about? They are all things God did for us. We were dead to God, unable to get back to Him, so we needed saving from the dead places – redeeming as Paul puts it. We have all gone wrong in life and I guess no one reading this would say they were perfect. So we are saved from those sins through forgiveness. God forgives what we've done. The little things and the big things. Kicking the cat and robbing a bank. Swearing at a motorist and adultery with a neighbour. No matter how small, it needs forgiving. No matter how big, it *is* forgiven. That's how big God is. How amazing His love. The extent of His grace. Grace – God's unmerited, unlimited favour for us. Wow, what a God we have!

We are so quick to judge, to grade sin, to decide what is forgivable and what is not. But the Bible tells us a different story. *All* our sins are forgiven. As far as the east is from the west, that's the distance He's removed our wrongs.[3] Have you tried measuring how far the east is from the west? I know where the north is- I can reach the North Pole. I know where the south is – I can get to the South Pole (maybe a bit of an effort, but I could do it!). But where is the west? Where does it end? How far round is the east? How far does it go? How do you measure how far the east is from the west? We can't do it. And that's the distance God has removed our sins. We can't begin to imagine how great God's forgiveness is. As far as the east is from the west . . .

And that's a good starting point for us as we start this book. How many of us have become more judgmental of our lives than God? Yes, it was an ugly sin. Yes, it hurt us, and others too. But *yes*, it *is* forgiven. Forgiven, forgotten, gone. That's why He died. He didn't just forgive the 'polite' sins, but the condemning ones too. The ones we dare not whisper. The ones we still condemn ourselves for. Forgiven, forgotten, gone.

I'm sure there are many reading these pages who know and appreciate redemption, forgiveness and grace on a daily basis, but right now, why don't you thank God anyway for His forgiveness and love, and ask again for grace for today? Go on, pray it now! Let's live our God-life, the life God has given. If we slip back into the dead places, He's there for us, waiting for us to seek Him again. To pray again. To find Him again.

Amazing though it may seem, we can never go too far from God. The Bible says if we go to the far end of the seas, God is there. Even if we feel we're in hell right now, He's been there, and He's able to rescue us.[4]

Linda's story

Her parents died young. By her twenties, Linda was a drug addict. She lost custody of her children and turned to prostitution. Working the streets of Southampton, she quickly realised that life was out of control. But running away was harder than you might think. Four times she was caught. Four times her 'pimp' beat her up, the last time putting her into hospital with a ruptured spleen. It was there that the ladies found her.

Two ladies had been regularly calling on Linda and when they found out she was in hospital, they didn't hesitate to travel the 40 miles to see her. 'Why do you want to bother with me?', Linda would say. 'I'm no-one, just a prostitute.' Their reply was always the same: 'But Jesus loves you.'

'I wanted it,' said Linda. 'I wanted what they had. But I felt it was impossible. I couldn't run, I'd only get hurt again. But then one day, I decided enough was enough. "I'm going to do it," I said. "I'm going to pray." The two ladies prayed with me. I asked God to forgive me and to change my life. He did. I know He did.'

The prayer worked. Linda came off drugs and this time ran away without being caught.

Now in Peterborough, Linda again found herself the wrong side of the law. Caught for drug trafficking, she ended up in Holloway prison. This time she knew it was serious. Either she changed or she died. Someone gave her a book:

'It was *Run Baby Run* by Nicky Cruz. It was all about gangs, drugs, prostitutes. I could relate to everything there. I read it in one sitting. In the book, God forgave and kept forgiving.

Inside that prison, I prayed again. And God forgave me again. He filled me with His Holy Spirit. Suddenly I felt whole. I had found who I was, who God had made me to be. Today, I still go back to Holloway – but this time to help other women, to tell them God can forgive the hardest person, take away the darkness, bring meaning, bring life.'

My own story seems a bit boring after Linda's. Yours too? It's not important. What is important is that we know God has rescued us from the dead places. That He forgives and keeps forgiving. We live with the cry of another country within us now. Like the boys of *Dead Poets Society*, we knew there was more to life, and we found that 'more', that God-life, the moment we found redemption, forgiveness and grace. We moved from dead lands to a living country.

I belong but I don't belong

Our story means that, although we live in this world, we don't belong to this world any more. That's what Jesus said. We may be *in* the world, but we are not *of* the world.[5]
  Here's how the writer to the Hebrews puts it in the New Testament:

> 'You've come to Mount Zion, the city where the living God resides. The invisible Jerusalem is populated by throngs of festive angels and Christian citizens. It is a city where God is Judge, with judgments that make us just. You've come to Jesus who presents us with a new covenant, a fresh charter from God.'[6]

The problem with reading a passage like that, is we tend to apply it to the future and not to the present. There is a future 'New Jerusalem',[7] but the writer is quite rightly writing in the present tense. We *have* come. It's here now. This is the new country. And when God broke in to our lives, we became citizens of that new country. Eternity has broken into the here and now! There is a cry of another country in our hearts, because we already belong to that country.

The battle of the time zones

I'm part of the generation that grew up with *Doctor Who* on the TV. The very first *Doctor Who*, I mean! My sister and I really did hide behind the settee when the Daleks came on! I love Doctor Who. Here's someone who can travel in time and because he knows the future, he can influence the present. He knows which direction the present should go in. And so do we.

We know the end of the story. So in the present we can do all we can to bring about that last day, the day when every knee will bow before the throne of God.

Rather like Doctor Who, we are involved in a battle of the time zones. The future has broken into the present, and we can influence the present so that more of the future breaks in.

The moment Jesus came over 2,000 years ago, the age to come broke into history. The future started breaking into the now. We live in those in-between times. It's the battle of the time zones. Every time the future breaks in, there are miracles, healings. That's why we see miraculous healings today. That's why we see many people accepting Jesus as their Lord and Saviour. It's the future breaking in.

As we look around the world, we see much that doesn't look like God has broken in. But even in the hardest of places, we can bring in the future. It's in the battle of the time zones that we need to remember to which time zone we belong. Or, put it another way, we need to remember which country we now live in.

C.S. Lewis, the author of the *Narnia* books, put it like this:

'I must keep alive in myself the desire for my true country, which I shall not find till after death; I must never let it get snowed under or turned aside; I must make it the main object of life to press on to that other country and to help others do the same.'[8]

Let's press on through, and help others do the same. As C.S. Lewis says, we will find that true country after death, but we already belong there. And in a sense, we are already there.

This is how the apostle Paul puts it:

'Each of us is raised into a light-filled world by our Father so that we can see where we're going in our new grace-sovereign country.'[9]

A new country. A new light-filled world. We are not yet in that country in a final sense, but the New Country life has started. God-life has broken in.

Out of the dead places

Now, if the future really has broken into the present, this has certain implications for our lives. We no longer need to live within the limitations of our old life. We no longer need to walk in the dead places. We have a different walk now.[10] We belong to a different country.

What caused Deborah to declare God's victory when thousands seemed to stand in her way?[11] The cry of another country. What made David brave enough to face Goliath, and at the same time to face an unbelieving Saul and an army that was laughing at him?[12] The cry of another country. What caused Stephen to forgive as he was stoned to death?[13] The cry of another country.

And what about us? Are we a Deborah, a David, a Stephen? Can God give us whatever it was that these men and women had? In the very next verse after Paul has talked about redemption, forgiveness and grace, he says that God has lavished these things on us.[14] Lavished! What a rich word. John repeats the same word in his letter when he says God has lavished his love on us.[15]

It doesn't matter what our background is, who our parents are, how much we own or don't own, God has lavished forgiveness on us. He's lavished His love on us. Lavish. Have a look in a thesaurus and see what it means: plentiful, rich, generous, overflowing, over-the-top, abundant, bountiful, copious, extravagant. God has extravagantly, abundantly blessed you. His love is bountiful, rich, copious. His forgiveness is generous, overflowing. The whole thing is over the top! It's for you and it's for now.

Now-power

If God has lavished redemption, forgiveness and grace on us, so we are now citizens of the 'new grace-sovereign country', then we have now-power.

It stands to reason. If I am now a citizen of God's new country, I have the citizen-rights. What are those rights? The ability to live God's way. The way He planned for His citizens to live.

When Roh and I got married, we also bought our first house. The day we signed the contract, the day we got the key, we were the new owners. From that day we had the right to live there. The right to sit in an armchair in that house. The right to light a fire in the grate (those were the days!). We were the owners, the key-holders.

God has given us the keys to the new country. We are entitled to live there. The land deeds have been settled on us, through the price Jesus paid. And if I'm in the new country, I have citizen's rights. Those rights mean I can be in the presence of the King of that country. To be in God's presence, to spend time with Jesus, changes us. Paul says this:

'We, who with unveiled faces all reflect the Lord's glory, are being transformed into his likeness with ever-increasing glory, which comes from the Lord.'[16]

As Paul puts it, the veil is no longer there. We don't have to cover ourselves. There is no shame. Unlike Adam and Eve at the beginning of time, we don't have to hide, we don't have to be ashamed. We can stand before our Lord, unveiled. Reflecting His glory, living the God-life He has for us. And as we do, we are transformed, we are made more and more like Him.

I know that one day I will be like Him. But the change has already started. To be like Him is also to be connected to the power source. If we put our hand in His hand, if we choose to live unveiled, then the power comes too. We can be a Deborah, a David, a Stephen.

When I was a boy, I joined the cub-scouts. We went away camping in a farmer's field. We were warned by the farmer not to touch the fence as it was electrified in order to keep the cattle out. I was only seven. Maybe if I touched it, it would be different ... The shock hurled me backwards to the ground! There was power when I touched that fence.

We know when we have touched the power source. We know when electricity is flowing through us! There is now-power when we live in that different country. There is now-power when our hand is in His hand. That power can flow through us to others.

Heart-written

A few years ago Roh and I had the privilege of meeting the Toda tribal people of India. They are an ancient Indian tribe, living in the Nilggiri hills. We were able to attend a prayer meeting there. What struck us immediately was that all the people there were women. In fact, the tribe is largely woman-led as the men have almost without exception become alcohol dependent.

Boy, did we learn what prayer was that day! They cried out for their men-folk. Sadly, the men, affected by the alcohol no doubt, often abuse their women. We heard one story that broke our hearts. One of the women from another village was not able to be there. She wrote to say that her husband had forced her to sign a piece of paper vowing to give up her Christian faith. He threatened that if she spoke of her faith again, he would cut her tongue out.

This lady wrote simply to say that she may be forced to write her name, she may even have her tongue cut out, but no one could ever cut out what God had written on her heart.

May God give us the strength and ability to stand in the way that lady did.

The veil is gone. We have a God-life, linked to a now-power source. We have the strength to stand. Have a read of this:

> *'It stands to reason, doesn't it, that if the alive-and-present God who raised Jesus from the dead moves into your life, he'll do the same thing in you that he did in Jesus, bringing you alive to himself? When God lives and breathes in you (and he does, as surely as he did in Jesus), you are delivered from that dead life. With his Spirit living in you, your body will be as alive as Christ's!'*[17]

God's Holy Spirit is the power source. It's the same power that was in Jesus. We are delivered from dead life and have the same power as Jesus. We are as alive as Christ! Think about it! That's amazing. God's power in you and me. That's God-life!

As we begin to realise the power that is available to us to live God's way, we will be further changed. And what's more, others will see it too. That alcoholic husband in India will see the truth in his wife's eyes. Our friends, neighbours and relatives will see the change in us. Often our witness will not be with words to those closest to us, but in actions and in reflecting the Lord's glory, as Paul puts it.

Nothing less

Having tasted of a different country, having enjoyed forgiveness and grace, having experienced just a touch of His glory, there grows within us a holy dissatisfaction for anything less. A dissatisfaction with the way the world is, with the way our friends live their lives. We cry out, 'It doesn't have to be this way!' It's the cry of another country. And it's the country of our birth. Our new birth.

Eternity has broken in. Eternal life starts now, not when we die. We are citizens of a new country. And the cry of another country is constantly with us. Eternal life now, living our new God-life, has enormous implications on our day-to-day lives. And that's what the rest of this book is about. Read on!

Notes _____

1. Ecclesiastes 3:11
2. Ephesians 1:7–8a
3. Psalm 103:12
4. Psalm 139:8–10
5. John 17:14
6. Hebrews 12:22–24, MSG
7. Revelation 21:2
8. C.S. Lewis, *Mere Christianity*, Book 3, chapter 10, Macmillan Publishing. First published 1943.
9. Romans 6:3, MSG. It's worth looking at the first verses of this chapter too – Paul says we have left the country where sin is sovereign and entered into a new country of grace!
10. 1 John 1:7
11. Judges 4:14
12. 1 Samuel 17
13. Acts 7:59–60
14. Ephesians 1:8
15. 1 John 3:1
16. 2 Corinthians 3:18
17. Romans 8:11, MSG

The Hot Line

It was the strangest of conversations. I could hear my secretary asking the woman to repeat what she was saying. Could she please speak to Ralph Turner? 'Yes,' said my secretary, but who was it who was calling? Number 10. 'Number 10 what?' said my secretary. 'Are you a restaurant or something?' The woman patiently explained that it really was Number 10 Downing Street on the phone! (I work in the pensions industry and was being invited to be part of a pensions 'think tank'.)

Well, it's not every day you get a call from Number 10, even if your secretary does think it's a local restaurant! I was rather pleased to note that by the end of the conversation, most of the department were listening in. It was a proud moment for me. It may only have been to do with pensions – but it *was* Number 10!

The amazing thing is we get a call from Number 10 every day. Our Number 10 is the hot line of heaven. We have direct access to God and He in turn does not hesitate to call us. If only we had the hearing to know when the phone was ringing...

Paul says that we've been shown a mystery – that mystery is that God has chosen us, even us, to know Him.[1] We've been chosen, we are part of His family. And He calls us up, wanting to speak to us!

God made us for fellowship, for friendship. He wanted to walk with us in the garden. Adam and Eve messed up that friendship, but eternity has broken in, Jesus has restored our relationship, so we can walk with Him again and enjoy a real God-life, a real relationship with God. Any relationship, to survive, requires that we talk to each other. So if we really want that walk with God, we need to talk with God. And talking is two-way.

Sometimes my youngest daughter Lois has had such a day at school, she just needs to talk. And talk she does. But it's two-way. I have to show I am listening, and I need to respond. Otherwise I get a, 'Dad, you're not really listening, are you?!' I wonder how often God says that to us? He calls us but we don't hear the phone ringing. We don't connect. God, who wants to talk to us, to walk with us, is left holding the phone as we go about our lives oblivious to the fact He's there for us. The phone is still ringing. Pick it up. He wants to talk to you, to share your day, to show He cares.

Albert Einstein said, 'there are only two ways to live your life. One is as though nothing is a miracle. The other is as though everything is a miracle.'[2] I wonder how many of us forget the miracles? We live each day as if God was not there, making Him a special treat for Sundays, when He wants to be there with us every day. To be there when we face that difficult exam, when we have to deal with the boss who is unjust, when we are facing a death in the family. And not just the tough times. He wants to be there when you score that goal in football, when you cry at the film, when you're out with your friends. He's a friend too. He made us to be His friends and wants to be there with us. Every day can be a miracle, walking with our amazing God, enjoying the mystery that is Him choosing us.

How do I hear?

How can I tell the phone is ringing? How do I pick up the receiver? How can I hear God?

The Bible says that we have been given God's Holy Spirit to help us. When we prayed that prayer, God came in and changed our lives. Instead of dead places, we have a living God. And we have the ears to hear Him. The disciple John says the Holy Spirit tells us about Jesus.[3] We can hear the phone ringing because we can hear with Holy Spirit ears.

Back to my conversation with my daughter Lois. I have to listen. Listening to God is just like listening to my daughter – before I can hear her, I must be ready to listen. I won't be able to hear her if I am talking myself, or my mind is distracted. So it is with God. If you want to hear Him speak, be quiet and be focused on what He is saying. Expect that He will speak to you. We have God's Holy Spirit living in us, after all, so it should not seem strange for God to communicate with us.

God may even speak audibly. As a very young Christian, I went on a special youth mission. Near the end of the week I was asked to give my testimony – something of a trial to a nervous seventeen-year-old! As I finished and collapsed in the safety of a pew near the back of the church building, the pastor of the church said, 'We've done a lot of talking to God tonight, now let's be quiet and listen to Him speaking to us.' God speaking to me – this was a new idea! I didn't know God could speak to me, so I fully expected to hear Him speak. And He did. I heard the words, 'Ralph, I want you to go to India.' I looked around to see if others had heard, but no, it was only me, and only for me. (Many years later, in an amazing way, God brought about the answer to His own words – more of that later in the book!)

Prayer can be a conversation, a saying 'hello' to God and expecting a reply. God may speak audibly, but often will prompt us through our thoughts or through reading the Bible.

God often speaks to us in visual images. The prophet Habakkuk longed to hear from God. He was so determined that he was willing to stand and wait for as long as it took. *'I will stand at my watch and station myself on the ramparts; I will look to see what he will say to me...'*[4] There was almost a visual looking for God to speak.

God was faithful in responding. *'Then the* LORD *replied, "Write down the revelation and make it plain on tablets..."'*[5] But there was an effort involved. There was a waiting for as long as it took.

King David was another listener, and like Habakkuk, he took time out to listen:

> *'Let the morning bring me word of your unfailing love,*
> *   for I have put my trust in you.*
> *Show me the way I should go,*
> *   for to you I lift up my soul.'*[6]

David's time out was in the morning, at the beginning of the day. Like a general in God's army, he wanted to hear from his Commanding Officer before he went out to battle. Beginning each day fresh with God is a great reminder that, as the Bible says, 'His mercies are new every morning.'[7] Find the time of day that works for you, but listening to God first thing in the morning is a great way to start the day.

Life-changing listening

Listening to God speak can be life changing. Just answering the phone and hearing His voice may change us forever. The ministry of Charles Finney, the great revivalist from the 1800s, started with a time of prayer where God met him in a remarkable way. Finney had been praying for most of the day when:

'I received a mighty baptism of the Holy Spirit. Without any expectation of it, without ever having the thought in my mind that there was any such thing for me, without any memory of ever hearing the thing mentioned by any person in the world, the Holy Spirit descended upon me in a manner that seemed to go through me, body and soul. I could feel the impression, like a wave of electricity, going through and through me. Indeed it seemed to come in waves of liquid love, for I could not express it in any other way.'[8]

I love that! Waves of liquid love! God is so ready to meet us, if we are prepared to set time aside to meet Him. He speaks, He changes us, He fills us with His Spirit. For Finney, it was a life-changing moment – it is the event he describes here that started Finney out on a lifetime of revival ministry.

Are we anticipating a life change when we listen in to God? Do we expect He will speak to us? Expect the un-expected! This is what that great pray-er Andrew Murray had to say:

'Beware in your prayers, above everything else, of limiting God, not only by unbelief, but by fancying that you know what He can do. Expect unexpected things, "above all that we ask or think" ... Think of your place and privilege in Christ, and expect great things!'[9]

Remember, the veil is gone. We are in heavenly places[10] and can expect heavenly direction for our lives. Expect great things!

Two-way communication

We don't just listen to God, He listens to us. He is infinitely patient, everlastingly gracious and an amazing listener! Unlike my fatherly attempts to listen to my daughter, God always

listens. Can you imagine if He didn't?! What if He was as
unhearing as we are? Maybe He just leaves the answerphone
on . . .

Here are a few real answerphone messages:

- 'Hi. I'm home right now, I'm just screening my calls.
  So start talking and if you're someone I want to speak
  with I'll pick up the phone. Otherwise, well, what can I
  say?'
- 'I'm only here in spirit at the moment, but if you'll leave
  your name and number, I will get back to you as soon as
  I'm here in person.'
- 'I don't want to bore you with metaphysics, but how do
  you know this is an answering machine? Maybe it's a
  dream, or maybe it's an illusion, or maybe *you* don't
  really exist. One way to find out is to leave a message,
  and if it's reality, I will call you back.'
- 'I might be in, I might be out, but leave a message and
  you might find out!'[11]

It's a relief to know that we do exist, that God is always in and
He always answers the phone! Here's the promise:

> '*Ask and it will be given to you; seek and you will find; knock and
> the door will be opened to you. For everyone who asks receives; he
> who seeks finds; and to him who knocks, the door will be opened.
> Which of you, if his son asks for bread, will give him a stone? Or if
> he asks for a fish, will give him a snake?*'[12]

He's a good father. He listens to His children and He wants to
bless us – but we have to ask in the first place. If we don't ask,
there's no chance of a fish *or* a snake! Like any father, God
knows best how to answer. There are four different ways I've
found that God answers my prayers – 'yes', 'no', 'wait' and
'here's something better'.

Yes

I guess this is the easiest of the answers. We pray, God says 'yes'. Gary and Jane are both blind. Despite their disability, they enjoy life to the full and have found that God has said 'yes' many times to many prayers. Whether it was enough money for a taxi, with a friend appearing at the crucial moment, or answered prayer for new jobs miraculously provided, God has not been slow to answer their prayers.

I feel it's a bit contagious with Gaz and Jane. You spend time with them, and you end up wanting to pray! They know their God answers prayer and they are bold in their own prayer lives. 'If you can't say it as it is with God, who can you say it to?!' says Gaz. 'It is said we only use about 10% of our brain power. It seems to me that it's the same with our prayer power too! Whatever the situation, it is just worth bringing it to God. This is base camp prayer!'

A few years back, Gaz and Jane were at breaking point. Being blind, they couldn't see what was happening outside their house and the local youths were taking advantage of that. It was not a safe place to live any more. But how were they to find the money for a bigger house?

'We did have some savings,' says Jane. 'We hoped it would be enough for the deposit on a new house.' That changed when both of them felt God was asking them to give the money away and put it in the church building offering. 'I must admit, once we knew it was God, we did it quickly before either of us had a chance to change our minds!'

It did leave them in a bit of a dilemma though. They needed to move but had no money. They prayed. On the very same day, two things happened. Gaz got a promotion at work and they heard that a couple in the church wanted to bless them financially. It was a significant amount – enough in fact, to put down a deposit on a house! 'It was one of the most incredible moments in our lives,' says Jane. 'We were just saying to God, "You know what, it doesn't matter, You are still God anyway," and the next thing we know, God has answered beyond our imagining.'

I'll let Jane finish this section just as she finished the interview with me: 'We disqualify ourselves because we don't ask. God has an abundance of blessings for us, but if we don't ask, we miss out on that abundance. We just have to ask!'

No

Hmmm. Much harder for us to cope with this answer from God, isn't it?! But when God says 'no' it's because there is a good reason. There is a 'yes' beyond the 'no'. There is a better answer, a different path. Ruth Bell Graham, the late wife of the evangelist Billy Graham, said this of God's 'no':

> 'God has not always answered my prayers. If he had, I would have married the wrong man. Several times.'[13]

It's hard at the time, but we need to remember we have a Father who wants the best for us. He sees what we can't see. He is the Alpha and Omega, the beginning and the end. So when God says 'no', when prayers seem unanswered, we need to remember we have a beginning and end God. We have a God who, as a loving Father, knows what is best for us. The Bible says God loves us with an everlasting love.[14] Love says 'no' sometimes.

Job struggled with this whole issue. With three friends around him who were not exactly good at giving advice, Job said in the end that wisdom cannot be found outside of God. Only God understands the way to wisdom.[15]

Sometimes we need to say the same. Only God understands, only God sees the whole picture. One day we may be able to ask the reasons why, but in the meantime, let's keep on believing our God knows best.

I must admit, I have really struggled with this one over the years. I think I know better. I think I know God. But I'm a beginner – we all are. God is bigger than we are. He knows more than we do.

Wait

Our timing is not God's timing. So often, we pray and we expect an instant answer. We live in a 'McDonald's' age of instant everything. But God is above and beyond our time and space. A day to the Lord is a thousand years to us.[16] That means that a ten-year wait for us is fourteen minutes and twenty-four seconds to God!

Remember, He is the Alpha and Omega, the beginning and the end. And because He is the beginning and the end, He can see what we cannot. He knows what is best for us. He knows when it's best to say 'wait' rather than an instant 'yes'.

Here's something better

It's back to God being our Father, our Daddy. As a child I asked my Dad for a scooter (the sort you push with your feet). He got me a bike. How much better! I asked for one thing, but got something much better.

Some years ago I found myself stranded in Hong Kong. I was in the airport and trying to get on a flight but things had gone wrong and it didn't look like I was going anywhere. I felt very alone. There were literally thousands of people all around me, but I was very lonely at that moment, not knowing what to do. Well, I did know what to do – I prayed. At that moment, around the corner came a friend from my church at home. I had no idea he was in Hong Kong at that time. There were thousands of people in that airport. There are 6.9 million people in Hong Kong. But at that moment, there was Dave from my home church. What encouragement at a moment of need! I was able to talk and pray with him, and a few minutes later the problem with the flight was cleared and I was on my way. God has a way of not 'just' answering, but answering abundantly!

Desire, discipline and delight

Larry Lea talks about us needing to desire to pray, getting on with the discipline of it, and as we do that, prayer becoming a delight.[17]

But how can I desire to pray? The key here is the same amazing fact we have already talked about. We already have a God-life. We have the Holy Spirit within us. We can't work up a desire to pray – but God can! Our desire to pray is birthed by the Holy Spirit. He helps us pray, even when we don't have the words.[18] Begin to thank God that He has put in you the desire to pray – and then launch out! Go on – take a break from reading (just remember to come back later!) and begin to pray. Remind God of His promise that if we ask anything in line with His will, He hears and answers.[19] And what can be more in line with His will than us on a hot line to God!?

Desire does need discipline, though. We need to keep going. I do a bit of long-distance running, and know full well that after a certain distance, usually at about 20 miles, you hit the 'wall'. Technically, this is a depletion of glycogen – but quite frankly, at 20 miles, I don't care what it is technically, all I know is I've had enough! I have to keep pushing through and, amazingly, my body responds and begins to find its energy another way.

In prayer, keep going. Even if you hit a wall (and if you are like me, my prayer wall is after about 5 minutes, not 20 miles!), don't stop. It passes. Desire gets you to discipline. Discipline gets you to delight. You want to be there. In God's presence. You find you are longing to get with God.

Go on. Thank God for the desire to pray, courtesy of the Holy Spirit. Discipline yourself to do it. And see the delight come.

A final word on prayer

I was told as a young believer to read books on prayer. I tried. And at the time, I wish I hadn't. I read that some great saint got up at 5.00am every day to pray. So I did the same. Then I read that another great saint felt he had to pray for at least two hours a day in order to deal with all he had to do. So I did the same. Then I read that another saint got up even earlier, prayed even longer … It all lasted about a week until I collapsed in a defeated heap!

By all means, encourage yourself with books on prayer. But build up the discipline in small, easily achieved stages. If you can pray for five minutes, try ten next time. Don't make my mistake and try and turn yourself into a super-saint in one easy step!

Notes

1. Ephesians 1:9–10
2. www.quotedb.com
3. 1 John 5:6
4. Habakkuk 2:1
5. Habakkuk 2:2
6. Psalm 143:8
7. Lamentations 3:22–23
8. *Autobiography of Charles Finney*, Bethany House Publishers, 1977, p. 21.
9. http://barbarah.wordpress.com/2007/05/03/thursday-thirteen-prayer/
10. Ephesians 2:6, ESV
11. http://www.goodquotes.com/answeringmachine.htm
12. Matthew 7:7–10
13. As quoted by Nicky Gumbel in *Questions of Life*, Kingsway Publications, 1993, p. 95.
14. Jeremiah 31:3
15. Job 28:12–13, 20–23
16. 2 Peter 3:8
17. Larry Lea, *Learning the Joy of Prayer*, Harvestime books, 1989.
18. Romans 8:26
19. 1 John 5:14–15

The Blood Line

I was standing there in the meeting. The worship had been good, but if you will excuse me for saying it, not that good. The worship leader started another song:

> Your blood speaks a better word
> Than all the empty claims I've heard upon this earth,
> Speaks righteousness for me
> And stands in my defence.
> Jesus, it's Your blood.
>
> What can wash away our sins?
> What can make us whole again?
> Nothing but the blood,
> Nothing but the blood of Jesus.
> What can wash us pure as snow?
> Welcomed as the friends of God?
> Nothing but Your blood,
> Nothing but Your blood, King Jesus.[1]

Suddenly, as we sang, the power of God came. It was one of those 'liquid love' moments Charles Finney spoke of. I could touch Him. I felt that if I opened my eyes, I would see Him.

The words were the catalyst. Right through history, there has been power in the blood.

The pre-emptive strike

The Bible is a blood book. It is a story of love and blood sacrifice. From the beginning of time, the Father knew He would have to send the Son. It wasn't an afterthought. It wasn't a reaction to Satan's work. It was a pre-emptive strike. It was the realisation from the dawn of time that nothing less than the blood would be enough for man to know God.

The Old Testament points back to that decision before time began, and forward to that moment in time when Jesus came and spilled His blood. Right through the Old Testament there are covenants – God promises – and many are in response to blood. As Noah sacrifices a burnt offering, God smelled the aroma of worship and promised never again to destroy all living creatures. He goes on to bless Noah with the earth and the animals, fulfilling the covenant he made.[2] Interestingly, God also talks about the preciousness of blood, demanding an accounting of any lifeblood spilt.[3] It's clear that God places a high value on blood.

God's covenant promises with Abraham are also responsive to the power of blood.[4] As Abraham shows his willingness to sacrifice his own son, so God promises He will make Abraham's descendants as numerous as the stars.[5] There's something about lifeblood that causes God to respond with promise and in power.

Painted over our lives

The Old Testament Exodus story is itself a pointer to a New Testament exodus – God freeing His people from Satan's slavery through Jesus' shed blood. The first Exodus – the freeing of Israel from Egyptian slavery – starts with blood.

As the angel of death visits Egypt, the reason he passes by the homes of the Israelites is the blood of a spotless lamb. That was the instruction to Israel, to paint the lintel and doorposts with the blood of a lamb.[6]

God is a just God. In justice, He must punish sin. And so with us. We deserve punishment. But the blood of a lamb has been painted over our lives. We have our own spotless lamb, Jesus. The Bible cries out in triumph that Satan is defeated by the blood of the lamb.[7] So when punishment is due, it passes us by. Jesus' blood spilled for us is the reason we have God-life.

God the Just demanded blood. God the Lover provided His own Son's. As an old Bible scholar once said, 'When man fell, he found mercy walking hand in hand with justice.'[8] Exactly.

The Passover, as the angel's visit became known, was an act of salvation through blood. It was that night that caused the release of the Israelites from slavery. Our Passover is also an act of salvation through blood. Instead of the punishment I deserve, God passes it over, because He sees the blood of Jesus painted over my life. When you and I prayed that prayer, asking Jesus to forgive us and change us, there was a blood transfusion. God no longer demanded my blood; instead He sees only Jesus' blood flowing through my life. My wrongs have been paid for through Jesus' blood.

A new New Year

I have an old vinyl record in my collection by Ron Salsbury and the J.C. Power Outlet. Yes, really. Really, they did call themselves that. And really, I bought it! It's the picture on the front that is memorable. The album is called *Forgiven*, and the picture is one of an apple with a piece eaten out of it, and that piece stuck back onto the apple with an Elastoplast. Nice idea. Great artwork. Lousy theology.

God didn't just stick us back together. He made a brand new me and a brand new you. To take the album picture, it's not the old apple with an Elastoplast, but a brand new apple.

Paul says we are a new creation – the old life has gone, the new life has come![9]

As Moses and the Israelites leave behind their slavery, God declares a new life, a brand new calendar. He says that as they leave Egypt, they are to treat it as a new month, the start of a new year.[10] There was to be a brand new New Year. Until that time there had been a different calendar, but now everything was new and everything revolved around a new date of freedom. When we prayed that prayer of freedom, a new month in a new year opened up for us too. We may still celebrate our birthday, but now we have a new birth day. Now we have a new start to a new God-life.

Pointing forward

And so, the blood stories of the Old Testament, each looking back to a decision before time itself, also point forward to the greatest blood sacrifice of all. Peter puts it like this:

> *'You weren't saved from dead places with silver and gold but with Jesus' precious blood. This was sorted before the world began and has now been shown to you.'*[11]

There is power in the blood. Power to save. Power to give us a new birth day. Power to make us part of a new country, a promised land. Taken from dead places, we have power to live a God-life. In effect, Jesus was slain before the world began. We were not born, but we *were* thought of. We were powerless,[12] but there was power in the blood for us. The cry of all eternity rings from the moment before time to the very end of time: There is power in the blood!

We've been made right with God because of the blood,[13] brought from death to life,[14] and it's wonderful! A hot line *to* heaven has resulted from the blood line *from* heaven. We know Him because He spilled His blood for us. The Old

Testament covenant promises point to the greatest promise of all. Jesus covenanted with us:

> *'This is my blood of the covenant, which is poured out for many for the forgiveness of sins.'* [15]

Back to that prayer I prayed as a fifteen-year-old. As I called out to God, as I asked for forgiveness, the blood that was spilled from before time became blood spilled for me. God promised, or covenanted, with me that Jesus' blood was enough. His blood was poured out for my forgiveness. One day I will stand before the throne of God and instead of all my wrongs being exposed, there will be a shout from the throne room – 'His blood has purchased you; enter in to the joy of the Lord!' [16]

Future, present, past...

The blood before time began dealt with the whole of my life. The future is eternal, the present is living a God-life and the past is the past. The blood deals with the past, so the past no longer has an effect on the future. This is important. So many of us find God-life and then live as if we have no hot line to heaven at all! We allow our past to continue to affect us, but the Bible says we are free from our past. [17]

Tea leaves and tarot cards

Zan and Annelle are South Africans and now part of our church at Peterborough. Both live out a clear God-life. And for Zan, it's been quite a journey. The child of 'Hippy' parents, he was brought up in a home that accepted the supernatural, but with an emphasis on New Age teaching as the source. Reading tea leaves and tarot cards was common in the house. It wasn't long before Zan was being strongly affected by 'spirits' that were definitely not from God.

He would wake up in the night, knowing there was something or someone in the room. There was a sense of being watched. Nights were demonically dark. Friends who visited would not stay. Zan's parents were aware of the problem but not the solution. One of their domestic helps turned out to be a witch-doctor and offered to help. But the 'help' made things worse. Some sort of poltergeist began to show itself, with pots and pans being supernaturally thrown around. The whole family were frightened. They chose to move house.

Spook house

The new house was in Namibia. It wasn't long before things were worse than before. Neighbours began to call their place the 'spook house', aware that there was a demonic presence there. Zan's parents were increasingly looking to New Age teaching to try and solve their 'spook house' problem. Mum went to see mediums and was on her way to becoming a medium herself, but again, all that seemed to happen was that things got worse.

A move back to Cape Town brought no solution. Once again people felt uncomfortable visiting the house. One day the evil presence was so strong it chased Zan out of the house and he was afraid to return. In desperation, they visited a 'White Witch' who instructed them to burn various potions throughout the house and garden. The family were crying out for a solution, but this seemed to produce even more of a demonic presence – and more sleepless nights. A friend suggested they visit a local church.

As Zan walked in to the church building with his family, there was a sense of a different sort of power. They were used to the 'spiritual', but this was a different Spirit. The Pastor spoke with an authority Zan was not used to. It took a few weeks, but it wasn't long before the whole family had found a new life in Jesus Christ. This had a dramatic effect on their home.

They prayed, declaring that God would have the say as to what came in and went out of their house and they began to notice a peace – the peace of God – settle on their home. They claimed protection through the power of the blood of Christ. In Zan's own words:

> 'The first noticeable thing to happen was a good night's sleep! As we declared Jesus' victory through His blood, as we threw out our New Age books and witch-doctor concoctions, we found God moved in. It's a lie that the devil is big – in reality he is small, and his power is in deception, making you think he's in charge. But it is God that's in charge now. New Age says you are what your star sign says you are. But as a family we found the truth – we are God's children, and as a good Father, God has much better plans for us. I used to be in fear. Now I have a destiny and purpose.'

There is power in the blood.

Forgotten power

Blood is an uncomfortable subject in the twenty-first century. On the one hand, we see so much of it in the latest violent films and video games. But on the other hand, to talk about being 'cleansed in the blood' seems distasteful and foolishness to so many.[18] And so it seems, even in the Church, there has been a lessening of emphasis on the blood of Christ. But when we do that we run the danger of becoming as bloodless as so many other so-called modern religions. Christianity is not a quick fix; it's a permanent God-life, and that needs blood.

We would do well to rediscover what the Bible teaches on blood and the central place the blood of Christ has in our lives. I love the way *The Message* version of the Bible puts it: *'It was a perfect sacrifice by a perfect person to perfect some very imperfect people.'*[19] The same Bible writer tells us that the only way we enter into God's throne room is through the blood.[20] It's the only way!

But what a way. *'We are completely free to enter the Most Holy Place without fear because of the blood of Jesus' death.'*[21]

Intriguingly, the Bible also seems to point to healing through Jesus' blood. Isaiah tells us it is through His stripes (i.e. the lashes He suffered on the way to the cross) that we are healed.[22] Some Christians take this scripture literally and understand that Jesus was suffering at that point in order to deal with sickness. Others take a broader view that points to Isaiah's scripture referring to the greatest sickness of all – sin. I hope you read this the right way, but really I'm not bothered which is the right interpretation! I'm going to let the theologians sort that one out and in the meantime claim those scriptures for my health and wellbeing. Whether they can be used specifically or not, Jesus wants us enjoying our relationship with Him and the Father, so let's have the good health that goes with that, shall we?!

Blood-life

Sometimes it's called communion. Sometimes, rather grandly, the Lord's Supper. Other times it's referred to as 'breaking bread'. Whatever you call it, it's an essential part of our Christian faith.

I remember my first time breaking bread (that's what my church at the time called it). I was encouraged to go by one of my friends. I'd only been a Christian a short while and had only attended the evening meeting. Breaking bread took place in the morning. 'You'll really like it,' my fellow teenager said, 'they use real wine!' Not the most obvious of reasons to go, but it did the trick.

Jesus deliberately took bread and wine before He faced His

blood sacrifice.[23] He introduced the breaking of bread and asked every believer through time to remember His sacrifice in this way. His body broken for us. His blood spilled for us. As we take bread and wine, that's what we are doing – remembering. As the Jews at the Passover remembered their salvation from Egypt, so the Christian at the breaking of bread remembers salvation from sin and death.

It's not only looking back, it's looking forward. As He broke bread that night with His disciples, Jesus was looking forward, beyond the cross. He saw salvation beyond sacrifice. There was joy beyond the pain.[24] And so as we break bread, we not only look back at the sacrifice, but forward to the end of all things, to the moment when this world is wound up, to the moment when every knee bows at the foot of the cross. We break bread and we look forward to that day.

The early disciples remembered and looked forward over meals in their homes.[25] We do seem to have made the whole breaking of bread thing a bit formal nowadays. The white cloth, the silver goblet, the form of words spoken over the bread and wine – where did they come from?! Not the Bible, that's for sure. Don't get hung up on ceremony, don't worry about having to say some sort of words as you break bread. God is concerned about the right heart, not the right procedures. Just together remember and together look forward, just as Jesus asked us to do. And if you don't happen to have bread and wine available as you are around your dining table, or attending your church small group, then make-do. I remember one of the most holy of moments was breaking bread at a Christian music festival. We had neither bread nor wine, so used cola and crisps!

Graphic

We talk about graphic video games. But Solomon brings his own graphic picture to bear in the Old Testament book of

1 Kings.[26] Here we read that in trying to capture the grandeur
of God, in trying somehow to record the power of God, to
measure what can't be measured, he and his people worship
God with the sacrifice of 22,000 bulls and 120,000 sheep. How
much blood is that?! Someone has calculated that just the
blood of three bulls would fill a conventional bath!

Solomon's worship, like others before and after him, looks
to the day God's Son shed His own blood.

The death of Jesus Christ, the Son of God, on a bloodied
cross outside Jerusalem is a graphic story and a graphic
picture. Without that sacrifice, there would be no God-life.
Paul writes in Ephesians that *'saving is all God's idea'*. And
*'because of Christ – dying that death, shedding that blood – we who
were out of it altogether are in on everything.'*[27] In the same
passage, Paul tells us that *'faith is now our home country'*.[28] We
are no longer strangers, we have come out of the dead places
into a faith-filled 'home country'. We belong. We know we
belong. We are in God's presence because of the blood.[29]
We are in on everything God has for us. And it's all the power
of the blood.

Notes

1. Lyrics from 'Nothing but the Blood' by Matt Redman. © Matt Redman, *Facedown*, 2004.
2. Genesis 6:18; 8:20–9:3
3. Genesis 9:4–5
4. For example, see Genesis 15:9–21. The promise comes as God moves between the pieces of the sacrifice.
5. Genesis 22:15–18
6. Exodus 12:7
7. Revelation 12:11
8. A.W. Pink, *The Sovereignty of God*, Banner of Truth Publications, 1986 reprint, p. 77.
9. 2 Corinthians 5:17
10. Exodus 12:1–2
11. 1 Peter 1:18–20, author's own wording
12. Romans 5:6
13. Romans 5:9

14. Romans 6:13
15. Matthew 26:28
16. Revelation 5:9, NASB; Matthew 25:21, KJV
17. Galatians 5:1
18. 1 Corinthians 1:18
19. Hebrews 10:14, MSG
20. Hebrews 10:10, 19
21. Hebrews 10:19, NCV
22. Isaiah 53:5, NKJV
23. Luke 22:19–20
24. Hebrews 12:2
25. Acts 2:46
26. 1 Kings 8:62, NKJV. This is not the only time of extravagant sacrifice. We read in verse 5 of the same chapter that so many cattle and sheep were sacrificed, they lost count! What worship!
27. Ephesians 2:13, MSG
28. Ephesians 2:19, MSG
29. Hebrews 10:9–10

View from the Balcony

We just kept climbing. The steps seemed to go on forever. Never one that was at his best with heights, there was a certain amount of queasiness along with the breathlessness.

But what a view from the balcony as we reached the top. Along with my India missions team, I had arrived at the top of the historic mosque in Hyderabad. A long way below (slight queasiness again!), I could see the streets set out in clear patterns. The market to the left. The main road through the centre. The bus station ahead and to the right. All clearly laid out.

It wasn't so at street level. If any of you reading this have been to India, you will know exactly what I mean. There seems no order at all at street level! In the UK, cars drive on the left. In India, cars drive on the left – unless they feel like driving on the right! Or maybe they want to do a U-turn in heavy traffic, or perhaps park three deep across the road. You drive using the horn and the accelerator. Brakes are for wimps. It all happens in India! Add to that thousands of people everywhere and you have a pretty chaotic picture.

But up above, you see something different. There was order there after all.

The big picture

We each of us face difficulties. In the turmoil, the emotion of
our lives, we can become disorientated. We lack perspective.
The problem seems so big, the grief so real, we can't see past
it. It's like there is a mountain in our way and no way over.
Stress levels are high and God seems small and so distant. The
patterns are gone, it feels like chaos. That's the moment to
remember to look through different eyes.

Dag Hammarskjold, the former Secretary-General of the
United Nations, said, 'never measure the height of a mountain
until you have reached the top. Then you will see how low
it was'.[1]

So there's the secret – looking from the top, looking through
different eyes. Climbing above and looking down. Easier said
than done? We have learned in the first three chapters that our
God-life gives us a Hot-Line through a Blood-Line. Because of
Jesus' death on a cross for us, we have access to God. In fact the
Bible tells us we can enter the holiest of places because of all
that Jesus did.[2] We can go right in to the throne room of God.
We can stand before the throne and not feel ashamed or
embarrassed. It's our home, our right, because of Jesus' death.
And where is the throne room of God? Paul tells us in Ephesians
– it's in heavenly places.[3] Above this world. Above the apparent
chaos. Above the problem. Above the grief. We are with Him.
We can look down, look through different eyes. And as we do,
we begin to see order in chaos. We begin to see God's plan,
God's perspective. The eternal life has come into the daily life
and we look again with new eyes. There is life, there is order . . .

God of order

Our God is a God of order. He can see things from above. He
can see the beginning and the end. He can see the patterns
when to us, at street level, it may look more like chaos.

The Bible tells us He ordered the stars. He set every one in its place.[4] It takes me ages just to organise my desk! But God ordered the stars, He even named them.[5] Scientists tell us there are about ten sextillion stars[6] (10 with another 21 noughts after it!) and even more planets. That takes some naming!

Just the sheer size of our universe speaks of the enormity of our God. I travel on business to the United States occasionally. It takes around seven hours to fly from London to New York. I travel in a jet plane that goes at approximately 500 miles per hour. If I travelled at the same speed to the moon, it would take me three weeks. If I travelled at the same speed to the sun, it would take me twenty-one years. The edge of the Solar System which our planet is in? 900 years. The furthest reaches of space, as far as our telescopes can see? That would take me, travelling at 500 miles per hour, around twenty quadrillion years[7] (that's a 20 with 15 noughts after it)! That's big! And God has set it in order.

He doesn't just do big. He's into small too. In fact He's into tiny … It is estimated that it would take one hundred million atoms lined up together to make an inch in length. But atoms are not that small. Scientists have identified the smallest known particle, called a quark.[8] And compared to an atom, they are really small! Imagine the new Wembley stadium in London representing the size of one atom. Now go to the centre circle of the football pitch and pick up one grain of soil. That's the nucleus of an atom. Then divide that nucleus into 1,000 tiny specks and one of those specks is about the size of a quark.[9]

Super stats God

And while we're on big and small, how about fast and slow? Powerful and gentle?

Sunlight takes eight minutes to get to the earth. But light from the furthest stars takes 12.3 billion years to get here.[10]

Yet God made the universe in a day. That's speed! He created
the sloth. It takes a sloth nearly a month to walk one mile.[11]
That's slow!

The Crab Nebula star blew up and was first seen in 1054 by
Chinese astronomers. It is still putting out 10 quadrillion volts
of electricity. That's thirty times the power of a lightning
bolt.[12] That's powerful. A breeze of less than one mile per
hour is enough to lift the dandelion seed. That's gentle.

How amazing that every snowflake is different. Every
flower has been individually made. We think we are a clever
lot, but even though we've reached the moon, we haven't
stopped discovering what God has made here on earth. A
couple of years ago, a whole new species of mammal showed
up.[13] Found in Borneo's forests, it's a bit bigger than a
domestic cat and has a long muscular tail. Not exactly so
small we could have missed it!

I was amused by a BBC headline on their web pages back in
2000. It announced that Jupiter had a new moon.[14] Not new at
all! It's been there all the while. It's just that we hadn't seen it
before! The Psalmist says,

> 'When I consider your heavens,
>   the work of your fingers,
> the moon and the stars,
>   what is man that you are mindful of him . . . ?'[15]

It can certainly make you feel like that. Just the vastness of
God's creation, the bigness of God. The detail He has gone to
in creating the quark and the fun He's had in keeping the
Borneo mammal out of sight until now! What is man indeed?!

Part of His plan

So then we come to it. The fact is that all this bigness, all this
order, all this universe that takes 20 quadrillion years to travel

through, all these quarks and Borneo mammals, have been made for us. Yes, really! How extravagant is that?! God has ordered it all just for us.

Before Nathan, our firstborn, arrived, Roh and I did a lot of work. We painted his room, we built a cot, bought new curtains, purchased baby clothes and endless numbers of nappies . . . Basically we got ready for the big day.

Before you and I were born, God did a lot of work. He painted the stars, prepared a planet, grew beautiful flowers, provided food to eat . . . He also got ready for the big day. We are part of His ordered plan. In fact we are central to His plan. Paul says in Ephesians that God has *'designs on us for glorious living'*.[16] He's designed the best. And we have the privilege of enjoying it. From the tiniest quark to the farthest star, all this is for us. The Bible tells us *'God cares, cares right down to the last detail'*.[17]

From the moment we get up to the time we shut our eyes at night, it is estimated we breathe 29,000 breaths. We blink our eyes 7,000 times a day and we talk around 16,000 words.[18] (If you're my daughter, add a few more.) And God delights in every breath. He hears our words and plans our steps.

When God said, *'Let there be light'*, He had you in mind. When He threw the stars into space, it was for you. When the first flower opened, you were central to His thoughts. As the oceans were separated, as life began, you were the apple of His eye. Part of His plan? Yes. Even more, central to His purposes. God says, *'Enjoy it, reign over it – the fish, the birds, the animals that scurry along the ground.'*[19] So let's follow Paul's advice: *'Please don't squander one bit of this marvellous life God has given us.'*[20]

Through God's eyes

As we begin to look at this life, this planet, this universe through God's eyes, as we begin to appreciate all He has given us, so we begin to appreciate every moment, every step. We begin to see the order in what at first seemed chaos. We begin to see God's purposes in our day-to-day lives. Life can seem a bit like a street in central India until you climb above it.

That this big God who made the tiniest quark cares for me is an amazing thought. That He made all that I see around me for me to enjoy is even more incredible. He wants me to enjoy this life. And the best way to do that is to see it God's way.

So the problem I face right now can be looked at through God's eyes. It can be seen as the momentary problem it is, in the context of an eternal relationship with the God of 20 quadrillion years worth of stars.

To understand how I can face my problems, it helps if I understand how God sees me. And if I begin to see 'me' the same way, if I appreciate who God has made me to be, then I can put into context the issues and anxieties of daily life.

How God sees me

Jesus tells the most beautiful of stories in the Gospels.[21] It's the story of a wild young man who runs away with his father's money. Money given to him, sure, but asked for ahead of due time. And money spent. The young man ends up washed up, worn out, tired, emotional, bankrupt. As he goes home, the father's response is wonderful. There is no hesitation, no second thought. The father runs to the young man, hugs him, welcomes him home, as if he had never been away. That's our God. We were playing truant, away from home. But He came running the moment we turned. We've all turned away. As Chris Lambrianou, one of the Kray twins' gang, convicted murderer and former prisoner says, 'We're all playing truant. It's just that some of us came back.'[22] We came back. And Father ran to us. That's how much we mean to Him.

So what does that mean to me when I'm at street level, trying to cope with the pressure and chaos around me? It means I'm loved. I'm His child. He cares for me not just in eternity but right now. He's with me in my struggles. He protects me. He prays for me. His arms are around me. He's my Father.[23]

God sees us so differently from the way we often see ourselves. Paul says we are *'more than conquerors'*.[24] I have to say; I don't feel 'more than a conqueror' a lot of the time. But it's fact, not feelings, that count. It's remembering the fact of who God has made me to be that makes the difference.

Janie is one of our Staff Pastors here at Peterborough. She has a wonderful way of greeting you as you pick up the phone. 'Hello, mighty man of God,' she says. And it's true. I am. I may not feel like it. But that is what God has made me. I can accept that label because of what Jesus has done for me.

Gideon didn't feel like a conqueror either. He was one of the puniest from the smallest of Israel's tribes. He said, 'I am the least and my clan is the weakest.' But God said, *'The LORD is with you, mighty warrior'*[25] Quite a difference of opinion there! We see ourselves as weak; He sees us as warriors! The key to God seeing us that way is in the same passage. God says, *'I will be with you.'* We are strong because He is strong. We are conquerors because He conquered all. Not only are we called back to the Father but we are sent out again, as warriors, about the Lord's work, in the Lord's strength.

Joel's story

Joel is a good friend of mine. Now a successful pastor overseeing around 350 churches in India, it wasn't always that way. In fact, Joel is a pretty good example of a prodigal running away. Let me explain:

Joel grew up a pastor's son, but as he reached his late teens, he rebelled big time. He joined an illegal movement called the Naxalites. The Naxalites are a communist type grouping in

India intent on fighting the current regime with bombs and bullets. Joel became involved at the highest levels and soon had a price on his life. He changed his name and went on the run.

Having arrived in Mumbai, Joel began to question this life he was leading. A wanted man, he was also a lonely man. And in that loneliness, he decided to end it all. He went to the central train station intending to throw himself under a train. The train came into the station. His heart was racing. This was it. The moment to end it all. Joel stepped out, falling off the platform. As he did, an arm grabbed hold of him. Pulling him backwards onto the platform, a man began to speak to him. What was amazing was that the man spoke in Telegu, Joel's local language, and not the language of Mumbai. The man began to speak to Joel about all he had done. Joel was confused. Maybe this was someone sent by his father to try and get him to come home? Or the police following him? Maybe it was a trap from one of the organisations wanting to kill him?

They went over the road from the station and sat in a park. The man continued to talk to Joel. He not only told Joel all he had done – some things only Joel himself knew – but began to speak of God's love and how God had a purpose for him. Joel was not to kill himself but to give himself to God again, who was a Father ready to forgive. The man went on to begin to outline Joel's future ministry and all God had for him to do.

As tears streamed down Joel's face, he looked at the man sitting in front of him. And there, right in front of his eyes, the man disappeared. God had sent an angel to rescue Joel. Needless to say Joel paid attention! He turned himself in to the authorities, served a time in jail and went on to do all God had called him to.

Do you really think stories like this are made up? Or just for the special few? The Bible says God has planned our days, He's in front of us and behind us, He's protecting our every step.[26] He cares for you so much, He's even there to help you to turn around and run again into the Father's arms.

He sees you as His precious child. Right now, fresh from reading Joel's amazing story, thank God in prayer for all He has done for you. Thank Him that He sees you as a conqueror, a warrior, and most importantly, as a rescued child.

Still He bends to hear us sing

So having understood something of the vastness of God, having learned how He sees us differently, having begun to believe that we are conquerors and warriors, let's look again at those issues that are facing us.

I don't want to make light of it. We can face some pretty big mountains in this life. But having established ourselves in God's throne room and now beginning to look down on the problem, we can begin to make sense of it.

Around 300 years ago, the saintly Madame Guyon was imprisoned in the Bastille for her faith. For seven years she was in a cell lying below the surface of the ground, with no light other than candle light. While imprisoned, she wrote the poem, *A Prisoner's Song*. Here are the first two verses:

> A little bird I am,
> Shut from the fields of air;
> And in my cage I sit and sing
> To Him Who placed me there;
> Well pleased a prisoner to be,
> Because, my God, it pleases Thee.

> Naught have I else to do:
> I sing the whole day long;
> And He Whom I most love to please
> Doth listen to my song:
> He caught and bound my wandering wing;
> But still He bends to hear me sing.[27]

Whatever we face, wherever we are, He still bends to hear us sing. What a Father we have. The light may have gone. There may be bars around us, but still He hears us, is with us, and cares for us to the last.

In the story of Daniel's three friends,[28] they faced going into the fire and losing their lives. Despite their situation, their declaration to the king who was punishing them was that God would not let them down. There was complete faith in God for the hardest of situations. And then they go on to say that even if God were not to save them, they would still not bow to the gods of the king. They continue to be faithful in a life or death situation.

Of course, many of us will know the story. Shadrach, Meshach and Abednego are met in the fire by a fourth person, *'looking like a son of the gods'* as the king puts it. He was there. They were rescued.

We may feel that, for us, the situation we face is as dark as a prison without light, as hot as a furnace without air, but we need to know He will stand with us, He understands. He's been there and He will be there. Still He bends to hear us sing.

God of the open spaces

Isaac was a man on a mission. The son of Abraham, the man of faith, Isaac wanted to obey God's call and take the land God had promised. In those days, the best way to stay in a place was to find water. No water, no livestock, no livelihood. So Isaac began to dig wells – and soon ran into opposition.[29] So he named that first well 'dispute' and moved on to dig again. Again there was a quarrel with the neighbours, so he named the second well 'opposition'. He dug for a third time. This time there was no opposition and he named the well 'wide open spaces', saying, 'Now the LORD has given us room to flourish.'

We have a God of wide open spaces. We can look through His eyes, over the mountains, over the horizon and see the wide open spaces He has for us. God promises us a hope and a future.[30] In Him we can overcome the problems we face, we can enjoy God's *'spacious living conditions'*[31] as Paul puts it.

There will be opposition. There will be disputes. But there is also a Father who embraces us, cares for us and sends us out to battle as conquerors and warriors on the victory side. As someone once said, 'We all live under the same sky, but we don't all have the same horizon.'[32] Whatever we face, there's a different view from the balcony.

Notes

1. http://en.wikiquote.org/
2. Hebrews 10:19–20
3. Ephesians 2:6
4. Psalm 8:3
5. Psalm 147:4
6. http://imagine.gsfc.nasa.gov/docs/ask_astro/answers/
7. As referenced by Sam Storms in *One Thing*, Christian Focus Publications, 2006, p. 90.
8. Strictly speaking, this is scientific theory – not proved as such.
9. Adapted from chapter 6 of *One Thing* by Sam Storms, Christian Focus Publications, 2006.
10. As referenced by Mark Batterson in *In a Pit with a Lion on a Snowy Day*, Multnomah Publishers, 2006, p. 28.
11. http://www.faqkids.com/
12. As referenced by Sam Storms in *One Thing*, Christian Focus Publications, 2006, p. 95.
13. BBC News Online, 6/12/05
14. BBC News Online, 23/7/00
15. Psalm 8:3–4
16. Ephesians 1:11, MSG
17. James 5:10, MSG
18. Referenced from Wikipedia.org
19. Genesis 1:28, NLT
20. 2 Corinthians 6:1, MSG
21. Luke 15:11–24
22. Interviewed in the *Daily Telegraph*

23. Jeremiah 31:3; Psalm 103:17; Romans 8:16, 34; 2 Peter 2:9; Isaiah 40:11; 64:8
24. Romans 8:37
25. Judges 6:11–16
26. Psalm 139
27. www.ebooksread.com/
28. Daniel 3
29. Genesis 26:19–22. See both NIV and *The Message*.
30. Jeremiah 29:11
31. 2 Corinthians 5:5, MSG
32. Konrad Adenauer, Thinkexist.com/quotes

Taking Hold

Solomon was having a bad day. *'Everything is meaningless ...
all things are wearisome ... there is nothing new under the sun,'*[1]
he complained. Maybe his bad day was to do with trying
to cope with some of his 700 wives?! Here was a king who
had allowed all around him to turn his heart away from
God.[2]

I guess he's right. There is nothing new under the sun.
That's if we choose to live under the sun. We learned in the
last chapter that our proper position is in heavenly places. So
we can live above the sun.

Solomon goes on to complain that whatever we achieve in
this life is of no use and when we inevitably die it's all
forgotten.[3] That's true too – if we chose to live and build only
for this life. But as we learned in chapter 1, we have eternal life
here and now. So we can live beyond the grave.

Living above the sun and beyond the grave. That's not
meaningless! That's fulfilling our destiny. That's living as God
intended.

We have a choice in how we live and what we build. We
can work hard in this life, but in the end it is all taken away
at the point of death. Or we can live above the sun and beyond
the grave, as God intended. And that means a stop to living
our way and a start to letting God have His way.

Letting go

Let's go back four years. I have a new job, hence a new car.
I'm on the M25 motorway, travelling in a three-lane 'traffic
jam' at about 50mph. Lots of concentration needed. Suddenly
the dashboard lights up with the code '2HR'. It's flashing on
and off. Sudden panic. What is '2HR'? Is the car about to
explode or something?!

So now I'm trying to drive and look in the car handbook at
the same time. The car is so new I have to take the cellophane
off the book first. Quite difficult to read and drive at the same
time! More panic, can't find a thing. The '2HR' is still going on
and off on the dashboard . . .

Eventually I find it. Would you believe I have bought a car
with a warning message that tells you to take a rest after you
have driven for two hours non-stop?! I certainly did need a rest
after that panic!

How many of us are trying to live with one hand on the
steering wheel and the other holding the instruction manual,
trying to guide ourselves through the traffic of life? The
sooner we let go and hand over the steering wheel to God the
better. Jesus is not just 'Saviour', He's 'Lord' too. He asks for
the steering wheel. Let Him drive. Let Him have all of your
life. That's the way to live above the sun and beyond the
grave.

God takes hold

It may be we prayed a prayer. It may be that, in a moment in
time, we responded to God's call on our lives. But the Bible
tells us that it's much more to do with God taking hold of us.[4]
So when we take our hands off the steering wheel of life and
let God drive, in some respects, He's always been driving. And
if it's not pushing the picture too far, He made the roads we
drive on, the scenery we pass on the way and knows about

every incident along the road of life. Remember, He's a big God.

He's an all-knowing God too. He planned the route, gave His own Son, Jesus, to ensure the drive is a heavenly one and sorted out the SatNav by giving us the Holy Spirit to guide us.

I want to talk some more about the Holy Spirit. We have learned that God has put a new country in our hearts, a new destination. We have understood that we have a hot-line connection with God through Jesus Christ and the blood He spilled. And the key to enjoying that new God-life relationship and making sure God affects every part of our life, is the Holy Spirit.

There are two famous Old Testament passages referring to the work of the Holy Spirit. One, in Ezekiel, speaks of an inward renewal:

> *'I will give you a new heart and put a new spirit in you; I will remove from you your heart of stone and give you a heart of flesh.'* [5]

That's what happens when we first receive God-life. God, by His Spirit, comes and lives within us. We have a new heart.

The other well known Old Testament quote, used by the disciple Peter on the day God's Holy Spirit broke out big time, is from Joel:

> *'And afterwards,*
> *I will pour out my Spirit on all people.*
> *Your sons and daughters will prophesy,*
> *your old men will dream dreams,*
> *your young men will see visions.'* [6]

Peter is using this passage to explain what was happening in front of the people of Jerusalem. They were witnessing Jesus' disciples being totally transformed before their eyes. This was the Holy Spirit coming on God's people with power. [7]

So there is an initial in-filling of the Holy Spirit when we first believe. Our heart is now flesh not stone. God has put a new spirit within us. And there is also a power outpouring of the Holy Spirit. Peter points to this as a second God-encounter. They are already believers, but had not yet been baptised in the Holy Spirit.

This is what Jesus had promised. In fact He had been insistent that the disciples were to wait for this moment of Holy Spirit filling. He told them not to start any sort of ministry, any announcements of Him being alive, until they were baptised in the Holy Spirit.[8] The disciples must have been excited. Here was Jesus, alive from the dead and in their midst. But Jesus contains their enthusiasm. He doesn't want them to go out in their own strength. In the end, that enthusiasm and human ability will fail. Jesus knows that they need a power encounter with the Holy Spirit. It really was that important. And if it was important then, guess what . . .

Don't live without the power! The baptism in the Holy Spirit brings power, you get charged up, you get strengthened and as the Bible says, you *'improve yourself'*.[9] With that strength from God, we can then go out, just as the early disciples did. Jesus says that's exactly what the baptism in the Holy Spirit is about – going out and telling others.[10] I'm not going to be able to do that in my own strength, but with Holy Spirit power, well, that's something different!

Then and now

'But I'd heard that the baptism in the Holy Spirit was only for the New Testament times.' It's an oft-used argument. But then we are still in New Testament times anyway! History tells us story after story of men and women filled with the Holy Spirit, speaking in tongues (which is the usual immediate result of this power gift), telling others and seeing many saved. Right through history we have revivals with power encounters with the Holy Spirit. One of these – what became a worldwide revival – started in Azusa Street in Los Angeles in 1906 when a semi-illiterate black preacher called William Seymour started teaching and preaching on the baptism of the Holy Spirit. Here's a quote from a visiting Baptist pastor at the time:

> 'The Holy Spirit fell upon me and filled me literally, as it seemed, to lift me up, for indeed I was in the air in an instant, shouting, "Praise God," and instantly I began to speak in another language. I could not have been more surprised if at the same moment someone had handed me a million dollars.'[11]

The newspapers picked up on the stories and reported 'hundreds of souls receiving salvation'. Soon, people were visiting from all over the world, and taking back the revival to their own towns and cities. The effects were being felt well into the 1920s and 30s. Many of today's churches can trace their roots back to Azusa Street.

Still laughing

Bringing it right up to date, let me introduce you to Brent, another friend from KingsGate Church, Peterborough. Brent had a tough upbringing, ending up in prison in his late teens. Upon release, he found himself in a church meeting where he went forward and gave his life to God. The pastor asked if he wanted more, to which Brent replied, 'I want all you've got, mate!' The pastor prayed again and Brent was filled with the Holy Spirit and began to speak in tongues.

What he remembers most, though, is the laughter. He started to laugh as God's Holy Spirit came on him. And I guess it's true to say, he still hasn't stopped! Brent's laughter can be heard in many a church meeting. He recalls the moment God's Spirit filled him. 'There was an incredible sense of joy.

Life seemed to light up in colour. Life had been so dull up until then. I was still laughing the next day at work. I haven't stopped, really.'

That's a long way round of saying that, yes, the baptism of the Holy Spirit is very much for today. So how about you? Ready to let go of the steering wheel?

What next?

If you're ready, and you're not baptised in the Holy Spirit, let's pray. Assuming you are a Christian, it's a step of faith that's needed.[12] One of my favourite passages is in John's first letter:

> 'This is the confidence we have in approaching God: that if we ask anything according to his will, he hears us. And if we know that he hears us – whatever we ask – we know that we have what we asked of him.'[13]

It's the passage I used to ask God to fill me with His Holy Spirit. I was on my own (being rather shy in those days I didn't want anyone praying for me in a meeting) and was just so desperate to have what I saw my friends had. So I read the verses and reminded God – as if He needed reminding! – that these verses must count for something, so how about baptism in the Holy Spirit?! I felt God's gentle touch. I began to move out in faith and managed to speak a few words in a heavenly language. And that was just the start.

So, go on. Ask. Receive. If we want to take hold of all that God has got for us, it's hands off the steering wheel time. Here's a prayer we can pray:

> 'Lord Jesus, thank You for the new life You have given. Right now, I agree with the words in the Bible that I can be baptised in the Holy Spirit. Holy Spirit, I invite You into my life in a new way. Come, Holy Spirit.

So, Lord, I have asked in line with what the Bible says. And, as the Bible says, I know You have heard. So I *have* received.'

The next step? Begin to speak out in the new language God has given you. Why speak in tongues? The Bible says it builds us up.[14] It can be used in a meeting but mainly it's a prayer language to God, worship to God.[15] It gives us a hot line to God in a different way. So go on, go for it. You may just get a few words in your mind at first, which are words you don't know, not from your normal spoken language. Be bold. Speak them out. It won't be long before there is a whole new language.

The Indian pastor Rambabu talks about speaking in tongues in prayer as being the phone line to God that only God picks up.[16] It's a prayer language, a supernatural language that God hears. No angel will intercept the prayer language. There is no pastor or priest that can understand it.[17] It's our own personal worship to God, our supernatural God-given tongue. So if, as we have learned, prayer is a hot line to God, speaking in tongues in our own prayer times is a *very* hot line!

Power encounter

As we see from that first baptism in the Holy Spirit at Pentecost, when the disciples were filled, the out-working was speaking in tongues. And, knowing they were now baptised in the Holy Spirit, the disciples began to move out into the community in power. Being in the presence of God had resulted in a filling of the power of God. The in-filling of the power of God resulted in a moving-out in God.

Baptism in the Holy Spirit is a power encounter for a purpose. Jesus expects that the disciples will, being full of the Holy Spirit, then move out and begin to tell others. That is the story of Pentecost, as the disciples came out of the upper room. That will be our story too. I can't speak to others about

my faith in Jesus in my own strength. It is God's work that
sees people get saved. And it is God's work in me that means I
can speak out for Him at all. If I have that power encounter
with God, I have the same Holy Spirit in me and upon me as
Jesus had in His ministry. That's quite a thought, isn't it? The
same power that Jesus had. In fact Jesus says we will go on to
do greater things than He did.[18] How can that be true? Only if
we move out in the same power Jesus had. That's how
important the Holy Spirit is. God *in* us from salvation, yes.
But God *on* us in power when we are baptised in the Holy
Spirit.

The results at that first outpouring of God's Holy Spirit
were there for all to see: thousands were saved and added to
that brand new church. The words 'added' and 'multiplied'
are used by the writer, Luke, on so many occasions in the
book of Acts. And it's all down to that power encounter with
the Holy Spirit. With God at the steering wheel of our lives,
with gas in the tank, it's an exciting drive!

We take hold

I'm excited as I write these words. What an amazing thought
that we move in the same power as Jesus moved in, in Bible
times! I so want to be full, and to remain full of the Holy Spirit.
The Apostle Paul encourages us to *'keep on being filled'* with
the Holy Spirit.[19]

Now there's a challenge – keep on being filled. Being
baptised in the Holy Spirit is not a one-off experience. Paul is
encouraging us to keep on being filled on a regular basis. We
need to. If I am only filled once and then I begin to give out,
the level I am filled to is likely to go down. I always want to
be full to the brim. I want to spill over the edge. So I'm going
to do all I can to keep full. Power encounters with God, yes.
And a discipline in my life that takes me to the Bible and
prayer.

He takes hold of me. And I need to take hold of Him. Paul says, *'I press on to take hold of that for which Christ Jesus took hold of me'*[20] My Indian Pastor friend Joel does a great preach on this verse. He says there are two types of 'taking hold', the cat and the monkey (keep reading – it will make sense!). The cat carries her young in her mouth. The kitten is entirely helpless hanging in its mother's mouth. The monkey is different. The mother moves around from tree to tree, and the young need to hold on tightly or they get left behind. As Joel puts it, 'God got hold of me like a cat; I get hold of God like a monkey!'

God's Word

To get hold of God, we need to get hold of His Word, the Bible. The famous reformer Martin Luther said, 'The Bible is alive, it speaks to me; it has feet, it runs after me; it has hands it lays hold of me.'[21] But for the Bible to do that, I have to read it! Want to know God with you through the day? Want that overflowing power of the Holy Spirit? Then make sure you regularly read God's Word, the Bible.

There are many helps to Bible reading. I grew up with *Every Day With Jesus*, a publication that is still around today. There is the excellent *Workman's One Year Bible Plan*[22] and plenty more. Maybe one of the best ways is just to regularly read from the Bible (maybe take a chapter from the Old Testament, one from the New, and a Psalm every day). As Martin Luther says, the Bible lays hold of us! The famous preacher from the 1940s and 50s, A.W. Tozer, referring to the Bible, said, 'I did not go through the book. The book went through me!'[23] Let the book go through you. Let it take hold of you. God still speaks today, and the Bible is a key instrument in His hands.

I travel to India on a regular basis. Each time, before I go, I take a course of anti-malaria tablets. It builds a resistance to

malaria. If any mosquito gets me, the resistance is there; I fight
back! I don't want to overstate the power of the devil, but we
do have an enemy. And should he bite, it's best to be
prepared. Taking a daily dose of God's Word ensures we
have the right resistance to the devil's infection. Like Jesus
when He was challenged, we know God's Word to be able to
deal with the devil's lies.[24]

Ernie has just finished an Alpha course,[25] an introductory
course to Christianity. He admits he has 'kind of known God
for a long time'. But recently it all became real. And not just
for Ernie, but for his wife Gill as well.

Having been involved in a life of crime in London, Ernie
came up to Peterborough to start again. With both Ernie and
Gill responding to Christ's call on their lives, it really has been
a new start. Ernie notices it most when he reads the Bible.
Ernie says, 'I once tried to read the Bible, but lost interest half
way through Genesis! It just didn't mean anything to me. But
now – now it's different. I can't get enough of it! The Bible
makes sense to me. I read it and I want to highlight every
passage! I was reading Proverbs the other day. What a book!
The 'fool' in Proverbs was me. I can see myself there the way I
was. It's as if God had put the words there just for me. I'm so
glad God has changed me.'

As I talked with Ernie, he proudly shows me a new Bible.
'I've just bought this one,' he says, 'the last one fell apart!'

Going for it

There's no other way to live. Letting God have the steering
wheel of life is the only way to go. We declare that in a
particular way when we get baptised in water. This is something *we* do, an outward declaration that we are going to let
God drive. Being baptised in water is much more than a
symbolic act of saying we will follow Jesus. It's a declaration
to the world around that we are going for it.

If you are a believer and not yet baptised, don't wait for a 'holy moment'. There's no need to seek guidance; the guidance is clear. Right in front of us. The Bible says *'repent and be baptised'*.[26] Simple as that!

Because we are obeying God, because we are taking hold of Him, we can expect that the occasion will be one where God meets us, and takes hold of us. Baptism in water and baptism in the Holy Spirit are two different things, but if you go for the first and have not yet experienced the second, then expect God to bless! Just as the Holy Spirit came on Jesus when He was baptised, if you are still waiting for the baptism in the Holy Spirit, baptism in water can be a great catalyst.

No short cuts

I remember running in the Fens a while back. I reckoned I could take a short cut through some fields to get back to the main road. Boy, was I wrong! I ran for miles out of my way. Whatever 'short cut' I took, I ended up blocked off from getting to the road by either water or a railway line. I had to go all the way back to the beginning and go the 'long way around', which of course was the shortest route all along!

There are no real short cuts in getting hold of God, in reading the Bible, in prayer and in time with God. But He's worth taking hold of. As He took hold of us, let's get serious in getting hold of all God has for us.

In the same 'taking hold' passage, the apostle Paul encourages us to keep running:

> 'I'm not saying I have this all together, that I have it made. But I am well on my way, reaching out for Christ, who has so wondrously reached out for me. Friends, don't get me wrong; by no means do I count myself an expert in all of this, but I've got my eye on the goal, where God is beckoning us onward – to Jesus. I'm off and running and I'm not turning back. So let's keep focused on the goal, those of

us who want everything God has for us. If any of you have something else in mind, something less than total commitment, God will clear your blurred vision – you'll see it yet! Now that we're on the right track, let's stay on it.[27]

So there you go. He takes hold of us, we take hold of Him. Like Paul, I'm no expert – but I'm off and running and I'm not turning back. I've got my eye on the goal – all God has for me. God's Holy Spirit in me and upon me. Overflowing with His life, moving in His power.

Jesus says, *'Anyone who intends to come with me has to let me lead. You're not in the driver's seat, I am.'*[28] Hands off the steering wheel. He's a good driver and it's a great journey.

Notes

1. Ecclesiastes 1:2–9
2. 1 Kings 11:3
3. Ecclesiastes 2:16–17
4. Have a read of Ephesians 1 in a modern version. See how strong the call of God is on our lives!
5. Ezekiel 36:26–27. See also Ezekiel 37:14.
6. Joel 2:28
7. Acts 2:3–21
8. Acts 1:4–5
9. 1 Corinthians 14:4, AMP
10. Acts 1:8
11. Rev. Ansel Post, quoted in Frank Bartleman, *Azusa Street*, Bridge Publishing, 1980, p. 61.
12. Galatians 3:14
13. 1 John 5:14–15. See also Luke 11:11–13.
14. 1 Corinthians 14:4
15. Acts 10:46
16. Teaching at KingsGate Church, Peterborough, 15/5/04. www.kingsgateuk.com
17. Speaking in tongues with interpretation is a different facet to the gift. I'm talking here about using our God given language in worship and personal prayer.
18. John 14:12
19. Ephesians 5:18. In the original Greek, 'be filled' means 'keep on being filled constantly and continually'.

20. Philippians 3:12
21. As quoted by Nicky Gumbel in *Questions of Life*, Kingsway Publications, 1993, p. 90.
22. *Workman's One Year Bible Plan* by Charles Sibthorpe. Using a colouring system, you read through the Bible in one year.
23. http://sacredoutfitter.blogspot.com/
24. Matthew 4:1–11
25. uk.alpha.org
26. Acts 2:38
27. Philippians 3:13–15, MSG
28. Matthew 16:25, MSG

CHAPTER 6

Breaking In

At this point in my life, I'm a London commuter. At 7.20 most weekday mornings you will find me down one end of Peterborough Station, waiting for the train to arrive, surrounded by twenty or thirty others, all planning to be first through the doors and first to find a seat.

I'm also a neighbour in a very pleasant part of Peterborough. Next door one way there's an accountant, the other way an investment manager. There's a retired car dealer, a fine wine seller, a civil servant and a children's doctor down the road.

And last but not least, I'm a husband and a father. I have a wonderful wife. The best there is. Four fantastic children. A Chocolate Labrador. A cat of dubious pedigree. A house, a garden, a car.

I'm grateful. Don't get me wrong, I'm really grateful. A wonderful family, a great house and a good job. But it's not enough. I'm not looking to change my wife or substitute the kids. I have no desire to move house and although Wesley the dog has his moments, I wouldn't trade him for anything. But it's still not enough.

For life to make sense, my God-life has to touch my daily life. I can't just be a husband and put my Bible reading in a different compartment of life. I can't just be a commuter and then turn into a Christian on Sunday mornings. Life has to be joined up. My faith has to break in to my daily life. Anything less and life is shallow and meaningless.

The great divide

'I have my work and I have my church. One is where I earn my living and the other is where I worship God. If I didn't have to do the first, I could do much more of the second.' Heard that kind of argument before? We are quick to introduce a sacred/ secular divide into our lives. But the divide is a false one. We don't suddenly become holy on Sunday mornings any more than we become secular on Monday mornings.

In fact, don't just apply it to work, apply it to the rest of your life. Is 'church' more important than the children? Than cleaning the house? Than visiting relatives? The fact we can think like that puts an incredible pressure on us. We begin to feel guilty for going to a football match, or drinking coffee with a friend. If we introduce a sacred/secular divide, we are in danger of trying to live as two separate people. And we become stressed when we are living in the 'secular', thinking we should be doing more 'important things'. A.W. Tozer puts it this way:

> 'One of the greatest hindrances to internal peace which the Christian encounters is the common habit of dividing our lives into two areas, the sacred and the secular ... As we are [then] compelled by the necessities of living to be always crossing back and forth from the one to the other, our inner lives tend to break up so that we live a divided instead of a unified life.'[1]

There's the choice. A divided life or a unified life. I want every moment of my life to count for God. I want my God-life to be my daily life. I don't want to wait until Sunday or Wednesday night small groups for life to make sense. I want all of my life to make sense. How about you?

God created work before Adam and Eve messed up. That's an important point. In Genesis chapter 2 God tells Adam and Eve to work in the garden, and it's not until the next chapter that they disobey God. The implications of this are immense. It means we can never consider work as irrelevant to God. It means work is part of God's plan, God's created purpose for you and me. Now that means I have to take a different view as to how I treat my day-to-day living. It means I respond differently to my boss, that I do all I can to work to the best of my ability.

Even if we are struggling with our job, God still has a plan for us. The Bible tells us that work has become hard because of our separation from God. Adam and Eve move from a beautiful garden which must have been a pleasure to work in, to soil that is hard to dig, with thorns and thistles and a lot of hard labour and sweat![2] Nevertheless, we can redeem our work, we can bring things back into line with God's intentions. Work won't ever be perfect this side of eternity, but it can be fulfilling. In the end, it is God who employs us. Look at this verse written by Paul:

> 'Whatever work you do, do it with all your heart. Do it for the Lord and not for men. Remember that you will get your reward from the Lord. He will give you what you should receive. You are working for the Lord Christ.'[3]

Some adjustments to how you look at your job, then? Don't worry, you're not alone. It is one of the least understood issues to do with our God-life. So many of us have struggled to make sense of the '9 to 5' and tried to live for the 'sacred' moments. But all it does is bring about frustration and stress. No matter how tough our job may be right now, if we give God the chance to change our thinking, that job will improve!

Coming to Peterborough

Let me tell you the story of how we ended up in Peterborough as a family. You see, if we had lived with a sacred/secular divide, we would never have got here.

I was working for a media company in the south of England. Roh, my wife, and I were fulfilled in every area of our lives. We loved our church in Crawley and were enjoying our growing family. Work was good, life was good ... But there was a nagging prompt from the Holy Spirit that we were meant to move on. The church group we were with began to move northwards, having been primarily in the south of the country until then. We began to pray about moving to the Midlands. I prepared my CV and sent it to a few search companies.

A month or so later, I had an interview in Peterborough for a large industrial company. As I drove to that interview, I knew that Peterborough was the place God was moving us to. At one point the road rises and you see the city below you. At my first sight of Peterborough, I felt such a peace from the Holy Spirit. I knew this was the place.

So imagine my surprise when a month or so on I heard that the company did not want to employ me! Back to calling on God. Had I got it wrong? I was sure I had heard God's prompt. I went away on business and took time out on the trip to pray especially for guidance on the move to Peterborough. I got back in time for a phone call from one of the search firms. I had not told them of my determination to only move to Peterborough, so was ready to turn them down. The guy on the phone said, 'I know you were looking to move to the Midlands, and this isn't quite the Midlands – it's a job in Peterborough.' I don't know if he realised how high I jumped off the floor as he said those words! This time the job was with another media company, so I was comfortable with the type of company, and this time it was a newly created job. The company felt they needed a benefits manager for the first time, as they grew. This time I got the job.

It was a bigger job and more pay than the first one I applied for. And it was created especially for me! God knows best!

My story fits well with our earlier discussions on God answering prayer. But it also illustrates the point regarding our God-life being applicable to all of our life. If I hadn't valued my job, if I hadn't considered that God was my ultimate boss in the '9 to 5' of life, I may not have even considered applying for a job that would stretch me and seemingly take me away from church activities. But it was this new role that got Roh and me to Peterborough and into all the purposes He had for us here.

And it's not just work. With God's help, there is no divide in any area of our life. So my interaction with my family, my friends and my neighbours is as important to God as my interaction with the church family on a Sunday. For many people we are the only 'gospel' they may know, the only link to the God that has changed our lives. What a privilege to be their friend, and with God's help to live out my God-life in front of them. May I never put them off knowing God, and may I always have the right attitude towards them.

It's a battle

It's easier, of course, not to apply our faith to our daily lives, our friends and neighbours. If we stay in our Sunday 'holy huddle', Satan doesn't much mind. But if we begin to allow God to break into our lives in every area, the resulting break-out to the world around will be contested.

The children of Israel broke out, escaping from Egypt, but because of disobedience and disbelief (provoked by the enemy of course), they were kept out in the desert for forty years. A whole generation died off before the next generation took the land God had promised them. God made just two exceptions to His punishment of the older generation. They were called Caleb and Joshua.

At the point where the whole Israelite community were rebelling against God, Caleb and Joshua called for calm. They were positive that despite the giants they had seen (the reason for the Israelite rebellion against God) they really could take the land that God had promised. Their secret was to keep their eyes in the right place. They didn't look at the giants in the land, they looked at the grapes. The Bible records it took two men to carry just one cluster of grapes.[4] That's some size! But totally in keeping with the way God does things. He promised a land flowing with milk and honey, so the grapes were never going to be supermarket size!

The Bible highlights three people in particular who kept the whole nation of Israel out from God's Promised Land. They were called Ahiman, Sheshai, and Talmai.[5] Just three people, but enough to stop a whole generation inheriting God's promises.

Forty years later, the story continues. Caleb, at the age of eighty-five, asks for permission to take the mountainous country of Hebron. He drives out the three giants living there – yes, you've guessed it – Ahiman, Sheshai, and Talmai.[6] The three giants that had kept out a whole generation were taken out by an eighty-five-year-old man!

The enemy will pretend to be fierce. Especially as we dare to speak for God, as we tell others the good news. If we look through human eyes, he can look like a giant standing in our way. But, like Caleb, we can look at the grapes and not the giants. We can look through God's eyes. And as we look from the throne room down on the mountain, suddenly that mountain looks so small.

When the world presses in

We are made to destroy giants. To allow God to break into our lives in such a way that the life He gives has to break out. But as this God-life breaks out, it's likely we will become more aware that there is an enemy of the faith. The result may be a bit of healthy persecution. The disciple Peter says:

> *'If you're abused because of Christ, count yourself fortunate. It's the Spirit of God and his glory in you that brought you to the notice of others. If they're on you because you broke the law or disturbed the peace, that's a different matter. But if it's because you're a Christian, don't give it a second thought. Be proud of the distinguished status reflected in that name!'*[7]

Satan is a fallen angel. It's important to say that. He's not God. He's not all-seeing, all-knowing or present everywhere. As a created being, he can only be in one place at one time, albeit he has many fallen angels working with him.[8] This is so important for our God-life. Satan is a defeated enemy and a limited enemy. He may claim to be a giant, but he's defeated. He will try and stop us following God and may well get a bit active as we get active for God. But it's putting things into proportion again, it's looking from above, from God's throne room where we are invited to live.

And when the world presses in? When things seem to go wrong? It's worth remembering that the maximum harm the devil can do is to take our life, but never our salvation. Pastor Paul Negrut, who was tortured during the Ceausescu regime in Romania said,

> 'The greatest threat and power that they have is the power to kill you. Our greatest victory is to die. So whenever they told me they were going to kill me, I said I can hardly wait – that would be my greatest victory. They will lose me forever and I will be forever home.'[9]

That's the context for us when we suffer. The Bible is clear there will be suffering for the Christian.[10] This is an imperfect world and the enemy will be keen to aim a few arrows our way. And despite the hot-line and the blood-line, we do have a way of getting ourselves out-of-line with God's purposes. Occasionally our injuries can be self-inflicted!

Aside from that ability to miss out on what God wants, we also need to be ready for enemy activity. The Bible says we are involved in spiritual warfare[11] and we are encouraged to prepare for battle! Paul says to put on God's armour[12] to protect ourselves. The Bible describes the enemy's activity as the *'enemy's schemes'*.[13] A possible translation of the word 'schemes' would be 'methods' or even 'mind games'. That's where the devil attacks – in the mind. He plays mind games with us. He is the accuser;[14] we get the blame for what we do wrong and even for what we don't do! But our answer is a simple one. He can accuse as much as he likes, but we don't work for him any more. We have a new employer, a new boss. One of the pieces of armour Paul talks about is the helmet of salvation. It's firmly on our head. We are 'saved', we are under new management. The old boss may rant and rave, but he has no authority over our employment. Our contract of employment is with a new employer, written permanently in blood. So let the devil play his mind games; our minds are protected. We may suffer, we may go through tough times, but none of this changes the facts – we have a new employer, a new direction. We live in a new country.

It is well with my soul

Horatio Spafford and his wife were still mourning the death of their son through fever when the great fire of Chicago destroyed much of what they owned. In need of a holiday, they decided to travel to Europe and meet up with their good friend, the preacher D.L. Moody. Spafford had business to attend to, so he sent his wife and four daughters ahead. The ship sank. Although the wife survived, all four daughters were lost. Spafford took the next available ship. As they passed the area where his daughters had drowned, Spafford quietly went to his cabin, got out pen and ink, and wrote. The words became the well known hymn, 'It Is Well with My Soul':

> When peace, like a river, attendeth my way,
> When sorrows like sea billows roll;
> Whatever my lot, Thou hast taught me to say,
> It is well, it is well with my soul.
> *It is well, it is well with my soul,*
> *It is well, it is well with my soul.*
>
> Though Satan should buffet, though trials should come,
> Let this blest assurance control,
> That Christ hath regarded my helpless estate,
> And hath shed His own blood for my soul.
> *It is well, it is well with my soul,*
> *It is well, it is well with my soul.*[15]

I don't know how I would respond to such devastating circumstances. But ultimately, it is well with my soul. Paul says the things we face are light and momentary afflictions compared to the glory ahead of us.[16] The loss of four children, possessions burned to the ground. Yet, it is well with my soul. I belong in a different country now. No matter what may happen on this earth, no matter how hard the circumstances, no matter how big the giants may seem to be, it is well with my soul.

God planned from the beginning of time to send His Son. 'God has landed on this enemy occupied world in human form.'[17] God has broken into our lives. The whole of our lives. Monday morning as much as Sunday morning. We may face hardship, even death. But our lives have been changed. God has come. We can never be the same again. It is well with my soul.

Notes

1. A.W.Tozer, *The Pursuit of God*, Kingsway Publications, 1984, p. 117.
2. Genesis 3:17
3. Colossians 3:23–24, NLV
4. Numbers 13:23
5. Numbers 13:22
6. Joshua 15:14
7. 1 Peter 4:14, MSG
8. Isaiah 14:12–15; Revelation 12:7–9
9. As quoted by Nicky Gumbel in the Alpha DVDs.
10. Romans 8:17; Acts 9:16
11. 2 Corinthians 10:4; Ephesians 6:12
12. Ephesians 6:13–18
13. 2 Corinthians 2:11
14. Revelation 12:10
15. www.cyberhymnal.org
16. 2 Corinthians 4:17, ESV
17. C.S. Lewis, *Mere Christianity*, Book 2, ch. 4, Macmillan Publishing. First published 1943.

CHAPTER

7

Breaking Out

I kept the video. From start to finish, there were six one-touch moves. From Brown at the back, to Rooney, to Carrick, to Heinze, to Giggs to Alan Smith – and it's in the net. What a sublime move. What a demolition of the opposition as Manchester United went on to beat Roma 7–1 on the night. That was a team at its best.

God has the best team for reaching this world, and you are a part of it. The team is called 'church'. He only has the one team and there are no substitutes. As I write this, there will be a number of pictures as to what 'church' is, appearing to a number of readers – not all of them complimentary! But church really is the most amazing God-answer to this world. Paul says:

> 'God raised [Jesus] from death and set him on a throne in deep heaven, in charge of running the universe, everything from galaxies to governments, no name and no power exempt from his rule. And not just for the time being, but forever. He is in charge of it all, has the final word on everything. At the centre of all this, Christ rules the church. The church, you see, is not peripheral to the world; the world is peripheral to the church. The church is Christ's body, in which he speaks and acts, by which he fills everything with his presence.'[1]

Look again at those verses Paul has written. Look at the order:

1. Jesus dies.
2. Jesus rises from the dead.
3. Jesus is in charge of everything forever.
4. Jesus is head of the Church.
5. Jesus speaks and acts through the Church.

No wonder Paul goes on to say that the Church is not peripheral (or on the side-lines) to the world, but it's actually the other way around! God's whole plan is based on the Church! The Church is central to the future history of the world. Jesus intends to rule, to speak and to act through the Church.

So what exactly is Church?

A friend of mine used a very helpful little phrase: 'Church is a family I am part of, not a meeting I go to.'[2] That sums it up well. For many, we 'go to church'. Church is seen as the building or the meeting. But Church is God's people – all of us, every day, wherever we are.

We belong to the universal Church worldwide – but that also has to have an outworking in the local context. It's no good saying we are part of the Church if we don't join a local congregation. The famous evangelist D.L. Moody was once approached by a lady asking to sing in the choir he used at his big meetings. Moody asked her what church she belonged to. In reply, she said that she belonged to the 'great universal Church of God'. So, as sharp as anything, Moody said she should go and find the choir director of the great universal Church and ask to sing in his choir instead! He was making a point of course. It's a cop-out to say we are part of the Church and then not be part of the Church in a local setting.

Here's Paul again, addressing a letter to the church in Corinth, Greece:

> *'To the church of God which is in Corinth, to those consecrated and purified and made holy in Christ Jesus, who are selected and called to be God's people, together with all those who in any place call upon and give honour to the name of our Lord Jesus Christ, both their Lord and ours.'[3]*

You see how he wrote that? He recognised a local church in Corinth, identified them as God's people and then extended the definition to anyone who knows Jesus as Lord. You have Jesus as your Lord? You're in the Church!

Anyway, as we're dealing with a church in Greece, let's learn a bit of Greek! The word 'church' comes from the Greek word *ekklesia*, which means 'called out'. We are the called-out ones, no longer belonging to this world, but with the cry of another country in our hearts. We are called to follow our Lord Jesus and in doing so, to be the Church, 'filling everything with His presence'.

One body

They're pretty bold statements of Paul's, aren't they? The Church through whom Christ speaks and acts. The Church central to all God's purposes. The Church to fill everything with God's presence. The 'called out ones', calling out to the world. Maybe we don't see that when we are together on an average Sunday morning?

As we saw in chapter 1, we live in an in-between time. Jesus has come and Jesus will come again. There's a tension there. We see the supernatural, but not in its fullness. We see healing, but not all are healed. We see a church, but not as it should be.

Is that reason to give up? Certainly not! It's all the more

reason to press on. If the Church really is central to God's plans, then let's do all we can to speed the process up! That means being honest with ourselves and with each other. We need to accept we are not perfect, and nor are our church friends. But that doesn't stop us working together. And the more we work together, the more we are changed. If we are brave enough to allow others to speak into our lives, we will see changes for the good. If we decide to hide away and wait for the second coming, nothing much will change and we will live a frustrated life, knowing there could be more, but being too afraid to take hold of it.

Let go of the fear. Allow your life to open up to others. Begin to be Church, reflecting Jesus, attractive to others.

The Bible says the Church is the body of Christ. With Jesus as our head, we as the body work out God's purposes here on the earth. The body has many different parts and all those parts need each other. Paul says,

> *'If Ear said, "I'm not beautiful like Eye, limpid and expressive; I don't deserve a place on the head," would you want to remove it from the body? If the body was all eye, how could it hear? If all ear, how could it smell? As it is, we see that God has carefully placed each part of the body right where he wanted it.'*[4]

I'm saddened by the number of times I meet people rather like the lady who spoke to D.L. Moody. They appear to be living off a diet of the God channel mixed with an occasional burst of daily Bible studies. Many have been hurt (usually unintentionally) by pastors with big feet. They have retreated, maintaining their Christian faith as far as they can, but with no regular contact with other Christians. It's like choosing a diet of fast food snacks when you have free access to Gordon Ramsay's restaurant at Claridges. In the end, cutting yourself off from the local church harms that individual far more than the pastor or congregation it was meant to spite.

Opening up

So if I need to be part of the local church, how do I begin to open up to others, how do I share that love and community that local church offers? Like most things in life, it's a step at a time. Find someone you trust (of the same sex) and begin to open up to them some of your fears and aspirations. Allow them to do the same. Join a house group (sometimes called small groups or cell groups), meeting in the week. This will provide you with the friendship and encouragement you need to grow in your Christian walk.

As I write this, we have around ninety small groups in KingsGate Church, Peterborough. It's one of the keys to our growth. We've seen 25% a year church membership growth over the last few years at KingsGate, with many of our new family finding faith in Christ for the first time. How do we keep them in a church with a Sunday congregation in excess of 1,500? Small groups are the answer. That's where friends are found and encouragement is given – both the arm around the shoulder and occasionally the boot up the backside!

To have someone who is looking out for you makes such a difference to your daily Christian walk. I go away on business quite a lot. It would be very easy for me, often literally the other side of the world, with no one to check on me, to do my own thing. And no one would know. But as I arrive at the hotel in Sydney, as I power up my laptop, there's the email from my mate Simon, checking in with me, encouraging me, and not afraid, when I return, to ask the difficult questions.

You'd kind of think that if you have a good close walk with God, you wouldn't need any other incentive to stay on the straight and narrow. But the 'I don't need others, I've got God' argument doesn't stack up. We are making things so easy for the devil to pick us off. However strong we think we are as a Christian, the support, prayer and encouragement of others is essential. The writer of the book of Hebrews (no one knows who he was by the way) says: *'You should not stay away from the church meetings, as some are doing, but you should meet together and encourage each other.'*[5] It's in the middle of a passage about us holding on, staying strong and avoiding sin. And then going out and showing others what God has done. That's what church is all about, building us up to send us out.

You want a strong walk with God? You want to enjoy your Christian life? Then, as my good friend and pastor Mike says, 'get tucked in' to local church!

What the world needs now

'What this world needs
Is not another one hit wonder with an axe to grind
Another two bit politician peddling lies
Another three ring circus society

What this world needs
Is not another sign waving super saint that's better than you
Another ear pleasing candy man afraid of the truth
Another prophet in an Armani suit

What this world needs is a Saviour who will rescue
A Spirit who will lead
A Father who will love them
In their time of need'[6]

They may not realise it, but what this world needs is the Church. It's the Church that introduces the Father to love them.

I was in Australia a couple of years back, at a pensions conference. There was a talk from Dr John Tickell.[7] Tickell's organisation has done a lot of research into what promotes long life (a subject dear to the hearts of pension managers and actuaries – people are living too long for their pensions to last out!). The research was carried out by interview, visiting some of the tribes and villages where everyone seemed to live long lives, as well as interviewing many individuals in their nineties and above. Dr Tickell began to explain that they had identified four things in their research which helped people live a long life. To help remember them, each began with the letter 'F'.

The first was 'Fun'. People who laughed and had fun lived longer. To have fun, you need the second 'F': 'Friends'. The research had identified that those with a big circle of friends or with a number of close friends were living more fulfilled lives and as a result, lived longer. The third 'F' was 'Family'. I couldn't help but notice that as Dr Tickell was explaining each of these factors, it sounded a lot like church. That's where I had found fun, friends and family.

Then the fourth point. Remember that Dr Tickell's organisation is not a Christian one as far as I am aware. So for a secular organisation to recognise that to live long you need 'Faith' was amazing.

Fun, friends, family and faith. Together they bring long life. That's what this world needs. That's what the local church can give.

People around us may look like they have everything together. They look complete, satisfied. Life is a party. They have no need for 'religion'. But begin to peer behind the painted faces and false smiles and you quickly find friends, neighbours and workmates crying out for the meaning to life. Remember, God has put an awareness of eternity into the hearts of men.[8] Without God, there is always going to be that 'empty feeling'. And that's where the Church comes in . . .

A beautiful shining reflection

Paul, writing to the church in Corinth says, *'Man was created first, as a beautiful shining reflection of God.'*[9] The first book of the Bible says, *'God made humans in his image reflecting God's very nature. You're here to bear fruit, reproduce, lavish life on the Earth, live bountifully!'* [10]

Oh that we would be a 'beautiful shining reflection of God' to our friends! Why not?! We have God's Holy Spirit power within us – the same power that was in Jesus. So with God in us, we can 'lavish life' on those around us! May they go away from having spent time with us with the thought that 'there is something different about them'!

That's exactly how my wife Roh got converted from Hinduism to Christ. She saw something different in her lecturer at college, the way she looked, a particular look in her eyes. She sought her out, found out what it was about her that was different and as a result found a brand new life, exchanging her false gods for a real one.

We learned in an earlier chapter that the baptism in the Holy Spirit is for a purpose. Jesus sent the disciples out in power to tell others the good news. That is our call too. But sometimes I can only reflect God. If I am with family, or with people I work with, it's not appropriate to always be speaking of my beliefs. They see me all the time and have to put up with me all the time, so it's not wise to push my faith on them. But what I can do, like Roh's college lecturer, is reflect the God I worship. I trust that in the way I live, how I speak, in how I work and act, they will see Jesus reflected. My hope and prayer is that they will want to know more – and as they ask, I'm ready to answer.

Bridges

What a privilege to be carriers of good news. In olden times, if a messenger brought bad news to a king, that messenger would often forfeit his life. What a relief that we have good news to bring! But how do we speak this good news? Should I be up on a soapbox in the middle of town, shouting out Bible verses? It may be right on occasions but may also show I'm

out of touch with what works. Or how about going house to
house with a Bible under my arm? Again, it can work, but I
may be in danger of being confused with Jehovah's Witnesses.
Paul says be ready *'in season and out of season'* to speak the
gospel[11] but I can do this in a way that is relevant and
connects well. Paul took great pains to ensure his relevance
when he spoke to the Greeks, using their worship of an
unknown god as a starting point, rather than just preaching at
them or reading out scriptures.[12]

Let's use the media around us. Let's communicate in
different ways. As a local church we can communicate
effectively not just through sermons, but through music,
dance, drama, DVD presentations, on web casts, pod casts,
email and much more.

For us as individuals, let's be ready for those conversations.
We can 'build a bridge' in our conversations and see whether
the person we are speaking to wants to climb on to the bridge.
What do I mean? Let's assume I've arrived at work on a
Monday morning and the person I'm talking to asks how the
weekend went. I might reply it was a great time, especially
Sunday morning when someone at church got healed (assuming someone did!). That provides a bridge for the person to
climb on to if they want and to start asking more questions
about it. But if they don't, that's okay too – there will be more
opportunities. We need to be ready, but we don't need to
force the pace. After all, it's God that saves, not us.

I mentioned healing just now. Healing is a wonderful way
of opening up opportunities to speak about our faith. Jesus
often healed first and preached later. We can do the same. If a
friend is unwell, offer to pray for them. As we expect God to
answer by His Holy Spirit, we can be sure our friend will be
back with more questions later!

As you know by now, I do a lot of work out in India. Some
of that is preaching, some is financing charitable projects. So
I can speak about the charity work to friends and work

colleagues and be pretty sure a conversation will follow. My mentioning the fact we help rescue children in India is the bridge. The friend climbs onto the bridge, asking what exactly we do and why we do it. That means I have permission to share my faith. And before long, my friend is crossing right over the bridge to the other side.

I remember one occasion, on a flight to the States. I was talking to the man next to me, building a bridge or two. What I didn't know was that the man behind us was also listening in. As we got off the flight, he leaned over to me and said, 'I know Him too.' How encouraging was that! It's so good to know we are not alone as we share our faith. Let's encourage each other and sharpen each other in what we say.

Broken and dislocated pieces

God's plan is worked out through the Church. He doesn't have to use the Church but He chooses to do so, through Jesus as head of the Church and you and me as part of the body. God has planned it all:

> 'From beginning to end [Jesus is] there, towering far above everything, everyone. So spacious is he, so roomy, that everything of God finds its proper place in him without crowding. Not only that, but all the broken and dislocated pieces of the universe – people and things, animals and atoms – get properly fixed and fit together in vibrant harmonies, all because of his death, his blood that poured down from the cross.'[13]

What a great way of putting it – God is about fitting together all the broken and dislocated pieces of the universe. Everyone gets properly fixed and fitted together in vibrant harmonies! That's the choice our friends, family and workmates have – they can choose to live a 'same old' life or they can live with vibrant harmonies. No competition! Paul says to get rid of the old and get on with the new:

> 'So don't you see that we don't owe this old do-it-yourself life one red cent? There's nothing in it for us, nothing at all. The best thing to do is give it a decent burial and get on with your new life. God's Spirit beckons. There are things to do and places to go!'[14]

That's the call to our friends. That's the call to the Church. There are things to do and places to go. As the Church responds to the call, lives are changed. God makes sure of that. Our job as the Church is to speak out. God is the one who changes hearts, the one who adopts us as sons and daughters.[15] Actually, that's quite a relief – we are not responsible for our friends' response, only for speaking out in the first place.

The Church in action

As we read the story of the birth of the Church in the book of Acts, we see the Church operation on a number of levels. They preach God's salvation. They care for the sick and look after the lonely, and many are healed. Theirs is a vibrant community, spilling over into the city around them.[16]

And so through history. In our own nation, we would not have schools and hospitals as they are today if it were not for the Church. Workers rights were pioneered by Christians. Many will recall the film *Amazing Grace* showing the life of William Wilberforce. Here's someone, as a committed Christian, working with the Church and changing the world with his combination of prayer and persistence. Because of his work, the slave trade was abolished and countless lives saved.

Today, from my own experiences in Peterborough, in this last year alone, we have served over six hundred families, providing furniture and food. We have actively worked alongside over twenty-five local agencies in helping the

102   *God-life*

homeless, the lonely, the poor. It's not meant as a boast. It's just, that's what the Church do! And not just our church, *the Church*.

In India my friends Joel and Blessy have been working among the temple prostitutes. Many women are born into prostitution, serving the so called needs of the Hindu priests. Joel and Blessy offer them a way out by enrolling them in a sewing school. Once the ladies have qualified (an official Government seamstress qualification), Joel and Blessy give them a new sewing machine and send them out to one of their village churches, away from the temptation to return to their former life. The women serve the local church with their work. The local church houses them and gives them a hope and a future.

Just a few illustrations. There are so many. Right through history, the Church has been a catalyst for change, health, healing and a better life.

Transforming lives

The Bible tells us we are God's *'special agents'*.[17] He has let us in on His plans. Short-term plans and long-range plans. And we are in on the action too!

> *'He thought of everything, provided for everything we could possibly need, letting us in on the plans he took such delight in making. He set it all out before us in Christ, a long-range plan in which everything would be brought together and summed up in him, everything in deepest heaven, everything on planet earth.'*[18]

The church is about transforming lives – from our neighbour-hoods to the nations by the power of God's love. What a calling! What a challenge! The Church effective in the home, the street, the city, the region, the nation and the nations. It can be done. It is being done! That's God's unfolding plan for the Church and the world. He has no other.

Notes

1. Ephesians 1:20–23, MSG
2. The late Richard Bartrop.
3. 1 Corinthians 1:2, AMP
4. 1 Corinthians 12:17–20, MSG
5. Hebrews 10:25, NCV
6. Lyrics from 'What this world needs' by Casting Crowns. © Casting Crowns, *The Altar and the Door*, 2007.
7. www.drjohntickell.com
8. Ecclesiastes 3:11
9. 1 Corinthians 11:10, MSG
10. Genesis 9:6, MSG
11. 2 Timothy 4:2
12. Acts 17:22–23
13. Colossians 1:18–20, MSG
14. Romans 8:12–14, MSG
15. Romans 8:15
16. Read the early chapters of Acts. Note especially Acts 5:15–16!
17. Ephesians 1:1, MSG
18. Ephesians 1:8–10, MSG

CHAPTER 8

Living on the Title Page

C.S. Lewis writes the most beautiful passage right at the end of his *Narnia* stories. This is what he says:

> 'For us, this is the end of all the stories, and we can most truly say that they all lived happily ever after. But for them, it was only the beginning of the real story. All their life in this world and all their adventures in Narnia had only been the cover and the title page: now at last they were beginning Chapter One of the Great Story which no one on earth has read: which goes on forever: in which every chapter is better than the one before.'[1]

We are only living on the title page. All of this life is just the beginning of eternal life. The God-life we have is going to go on through all of time and eternity. As it is, we get glimpses of reality – points at which the future of eternity has broken into the now of the present. That means our 'title pages' can be wonderfully coloured, reflecting the eternal to come. That means we can enjoy eternal life now. We can colour our life, enjoy the best that God has got for us. Here's what the Psalmist says:

> *'My frame was not hidden from You when I was being formed in secret [and] intricately and curiously wrought [as if embroidered with various colours]'*[2]

That's God's intention, to colour us, to embroider colours into our lives, to make out of us 'vibrant harmonies',[3] as Paul puts it. I *so* want that for my life. You too? It's possible if we put God first.

I'm typing this book on a laptop. Every now and again, as I take a break, the screensaver comes on. It shows my holiday snaps mostly. There are a few photos on there from my friend Zan when we went on holiday together. Unlike me, Zan is a very good photographer. The photo that just came up is one of a sunset over Snowdonia. Such magnificent colours: reds, oranges, purples, all highlighting the curve of the mountains, the colours of the hills. Such brilliance. Jesus says if God knows how to clothe the flowers of the field in such beauty, how much more will He care for us.[4] How much more will he embroider and colour our lives!

The pursuit of happiness

So, what do I colour my life with? The theologian John Piper argues that God is most glorified when we are most satisfied in Him. Piper says that 'pursuing the highest good will always result in our greatest happiness in the end. We should pursue this happiness, and pursue it with all our might.'[5] We should aim to be happy. That's a good thing to aim for. In fact many people in the world today would agree that happiness is what we *should* aim for. But happiness will always be found most in our pursuit of God. When we put Him first, we are satisfied. When we are satisfied, then we are happy and God is glorified in our lives.

Any other pursuit, however noble, will not result in that same satisfaction or happiness, the same colour in our lives. But when God comes first, all that we do is reflected through that relationship. I can enjoy my family, my job, my hobbies and my friends more when God is first in my life. I can genuinely be happy. It may only be the title page, but this life is to be enjoyed!

Does that mean I should pretend to be enjoying life when things go wrong? No, let's not pretend or wear a mask. There is nothing duller than the super-religious person pretending all is well with the world when they know full well it's just a mask put on to fool people.

We have learned that, with God's help, we can look at problems in a different way. We can see beyond the cover page. And that does help us deal with the hard times. The Bible talks about our suffering[6] but even in hard times it seems to me we can let eternity shine through and colour our lives. So I don't pretend that things are not hard, but I do look beyond the moment of hardship and see how God has blessed me with God-life in the here and now.

Paul says,

> 'We do not look at the things that can be seen. We look at the things that cannot be seen. The things that can be seen will come to an end. But the things that cannot be seen will last forever.'[7]

A glimpse of reality

In Paul's first letter to Corinth, he writes that we only see things in shadows at the moment but one day we will see Him face to face.[8] I believe the nearest we get to seeing God face to face in this life is as we worship Him. The weather clears and the sun shines bright. No more shadows, no more mist. For a moment in worship, we see Him. It's a glimpse of reality.

Paul encourages us to present our bodies as a spiritual sacrifice in worship.[9] In other words, it's not about me, it's all about Him. Sometimes people can get a bit caught up with where to worship, what type of music should be playing or how worship might look to others. What is most important is how it looks to God.

Worship is much more than a song of course. It can include prayer, reading the Bible, breaking bread together, and even serving others practically. It's our sacrifice to God. It's for Him. Someone once complained to their pastor that they didn't get much out of the worship that morning. 'That's okay,' said the pastor with a smile. 'What do you mean, that's okay?' said the church member, getting more and more irate. 'It's not good enough. I'm not getting anything out of these worship times.' 'But,' said the pastor, 'it's not for you. It's not what you get out of it. It's what He gets out of it. Worship is for God not for you.' Well said!

One of the most beautiful pictures of worship in the Bible is that of a woman pouring perfume over Jesus.[10] It's just a few days before Jesus goes to the cross and Jesus actually says it's in preparation for his burial. The perfume is expensive and fragrant. It is likely that the smell on His hair and skin would remain for several days. In other words, as Jesus hung on the cross, He could still smell the worship of that woman. We saw earlier that Jesus saw the joy beyond the pain as He went to the cross. At that moment He smelt it too.

And that's why we worship of course. It's back to the blood again. Worship is for Him, because He is worth it. It doesn't matter what others think. It doesn't matter whether we get anything out of it. He deserves it.

But God is so generous – as we touch Him, we see Him. It's for Him, but we are caught up in worship and see that glimpse of reality beyond the title page. It thrills us to be in His presence. It colours our life. It satisfies us. And God is most glorified when we are most satisfied in Him.

The day will come

There will be a day. A day of judgment and a day of worship like no other, when every knee will bow and every tongue confess that Jesus is Lord.[11] What we see in part today will be seen in all its fullness. The eternal breakthrough we have experienced in this life will become eternity, God with us for ever.

Everyone will be there on that day. Every prime minister and president. Every king and queen, every lord and lady through history. The great and the good. The tyrant and the traitor. Hitler, Napoleon, Churchill and Thatcher. Ghandi, Mandela, Sadaam and Mugabe. Christians, Moslems, Sikhs and Hindus. All will bow the knee on that day. All will be judged.[12] There will be a separation between those that know God through Jesus Christ and those that don't.[13] And for those of us who have God-life, for those of us who prayed a prayer and know God's life in us, there will be no judgment to hell. There will be no list of all we have done wrong held in evidence against us. Instead there will be an opening of a book; the book of life.[14] Our names will be there, written in Jesus' blood.

What a day. An end to this life. An end to the title page. The beginning of the book itself.

Things to do and places to go

We look forward to that day. And we live in the light of that day. In the meantime there is a job to do. Let's have a look at that passage from Romans again:

> 'Don't you see that we don't owe this old do-it-yourself life one red cent? There's nothing in it for us, nothing at all. The best thing to do is give it a decent burial and get on with your new life. God's Spirit beckons. There are things to do and places to go!'[15]

There are things to do and places to go! So let's go and do!

One of the most famous Bible quotes is Jesus' 'Great Commission'. Before He goes back to heaven, having risen from the dead, He instructs his disciples with His final words

in the Gospel of Matthew. He is sending the disciples out (and
that includes you and me). This is what He says:

> *'All authority in heaven and on earth has been given to me.
> Therefore go and make disciples of all nations, baptizing them in the
> name of the Father and of the Son and of the Holy Spirit, and
> teaching them to obey everything I have commanded you. And surely
> I am with you always, to the very end of the age.'*[16]

Jesus says there is a 'very end of the age' to come, the day
when all will bow the knee. But in the meantime there is a job
to do – things to do, places to go. And that's not an option, it's
an instruction. As someone once said, it's the 'Great Commission', not the 'Great Suggestion'! But as we go, He is with us.
We go in the power of the Holy Spirit. Here are some more of
Jesus' final words:

> *'You will receive power when the Holy Spirit comes on you; and you
> will be my witnesses in Jerusalem, and in all Judea and Samaria,
> and to the ends of the earth.'*[17]

We are not on our own. This 'Great Commission' has great
power. The power of the Holy Spirit is with us as we go. God
has planned the 'things to do and places to go' so we can
expect success. We work for continued eternal breakthrough
until the final eternal day.

Signposts to another country

It's true. We are not on our own. God is with us. We have
the Holy Spirit within us. And we have what chapter 12 of the
Hebrews letter calls a *'great cloud of witnesses'* cheering us on.[18]
The chapter before lists many of them. Heroes and heroines,
every one of them. They walked God's ways and fought for
God's ways. Some triumphed. Others were sawn in two.

Some shut the mouths of lions, others were tortured for their faith.

It's not what happened to them. It's that they persevered. They kept going, no matter what. And they received God's commendation, God's 'well done'.

They have gone before us. They are our example. Abel, Enoch, Noah. Abraham, Isaac, Jacob. Moses, Joshua, Rahab. Everyone a hero. Not perfect. Not always ensuring the hotline to heaven is open. Not always listening and obeying. In fact, quite like us really.

And now they cheer us on. The have walked the same path as us. Followed the same signposts to another country.

It's not just the Bible heroes of course. History is full of faithful men and women who have followed the same signposts. Men like Charles Finney, D.L. Moody or Billy Graham who saw great crowds swept into the kingdom in their meetings. Missionaries like William Carey, David Livingstone or Hudson Taylor, giving their whole lives for people at the other end of the world. Men of revival such as John Wesley, George Whitefield and, in more recent times, Duncan Campbell. Those who gave their lives – like the people listed in Hebrews, often seemingly without immediate fruit to show for it – such as Jim Elliot, John and Betty Stamm or Cassie Bernall who died in the Columbine College shootings. They have all gone before us. They all cheer us on.

(By the way, was that just a list of names to you? They are all heroes of our faith. So your homework . . . look up some of the names on the internet and see what you find!)

Same path, different footsteps

Right from Abraham, via the early disciples, through history, to these present times, people have trodden the same road as us. Same path, different footsteps.

Jim Elliot died in 1956 aged twenty-eight. He was killed by the South American Indians he was trying to reach for the gospel. This is what he recorded in his journal:

> 'He is no fool who gives what he cannot keep, to gain what he cannot lose.'[19]

Think about it. We can't keep this present life. In the end we die. So let's go for it, to gain what we can't lose. Cassie Bernall did that. As the young student gunman aimed a gun at her head and asked if she was a Christian, she knew she might lose her life with the wrong answer. She said 'yes'. That was the moment she died. A waste of a life? This is what she wrote just a week before her death:

> 'Whatever it takes I will be one who lives in the fresh newness of life of those who are alive from the dead.'[20]

She did.

So, Jim and Cassie, together with all the believers through history, cheer us on. But Hebrews says that they didn't get God's full promise:

> *'Not one of these people, even though their lives of faith were exemplary, got their hands on what was promised. God had a better plan for us: that their faith and our faith would come together to make one completed whole, their lives of faith not complete apart from ours.'*[21]

That's it! Our lives together tell the whole story. None of us on our own can tell it. The writer goes on:

> *'Do you see what this means – all these pioneers who blazed the way, all these veterans cheering us on? It means we'd better get on with it. Strip down, start running – and never quit! No extra spiritual fat, no*

parasitic sins. Keep your eyes on Jesus, who both began and finished this race we're in. Study how he did it. Because he never lost sight of where he was heading – that exhilarating finish in and with God – he could put up with anything along the way: Cross, shame, whatever. And now he's there, in the place of honour, right alongside God. When you find yourselves flagging in your faith, go over that story again, item by item, that long litany of hostility he ploughed through. That will shoot adrenaline into your souls!'[22]

What wonderful words. Keep running. Never quit. If we stumble, let's keep our eyes on Jesus, who never lost sight of where He was going. And if we do find we get tired, go over the story again. Read this book, better still, read the Bible. Again. Item by item. Story by story. Allow God through His Word to shoot adrenaline into us!

The time is now

We only have one life. One moment in time to affect history. We have one decision to make – whether to affect history or to just watch it go by. I never was one for sitting on the sidelines. How about you? Let's go for all God has got for us, living life to the full. Enjoying God, putting Him first.

We keep a phone in our bedroom, just in case. It went off one night at about 2.30am. The moment it rang, I leapt out of bed. There were hundreds of thoughts going through my head. Who was ill? Who had died? What was the emergency?

I picked up the phone. It was Blessy, our friend in India. 'Hello, brother Ralph, how are you?' 'Fine, thanks, Blessy. What's the matter, is everything alright?' 'Yes, fine thank you brother. And how is sister Rohini?' 'Fine, thanks, Blessy'. At this point she began to realise that my voice was somewhat strained. 'What time is it there, brother?' 'Blessy, it's 2.30 in the morning!' 'Oh. Oh, I'm so sorry. I must have counted the hours the wrong way!'

Very funny – and I love teasing Blessy about it, but let's not get the time wrong. We live once. Let's make sure every hour counts. Our friends and neighbours need to hear about Jesus. The time is now. We're in the race. Keep running.

God has a way of calling us on and into all He has for us. Remember I told you about the time God spoke audibly to me about going to India? A few years later, I met and married Roh. As she is Indian, I decided that fulfilled the call. Roh was my India, I didn't have to go anywhere! Twenty-six years after God spoke to me about India, Roh and I found ourselves in a Christian meeting. The person leading invited anyone with a heart for India to come to the front. Roh and I went, expecting we would be asked to pray for that country. The next thing we know, someone is prophesying over us and sending us out there! We may forget God's call on our lives. He does not.

God directs. Keep running. And keep dreaming:

> 'All men dream: but not equally. Those who dream by night in the dusty recesses of their minds wake in the day to find that it was vanity: but the dreamers of the day are dangerous men, for they may act their dreams with open eyes, to make it possible.'[23]

Like Lawrence of Arabia, the author of that quote, I want to dream in the daytime. I want to be dangerous, to act out my God-given dreams, to make it possible.

A time for heroes

The eleventh chapter of Hebrews is there for a reason. It's not just a list. It's there to inspire us. It tells us in chapter 12 that all the people listed and more through history are cheering us on to our own exploits. It's a list of heroes and heroines. And it's a list of ordinary people doing extraordinary things for God.

Most heroes will tell you they never intended to be. They were just there at the right time. I remember the man who helped so many to safety from Aldgate the day the terrorists hit the tube lines in London. He was just there. He acted to help, not to be a hero.

As a family we went to the Norfolk coast for a holiday. Near to Cromer there is a statue to Henry Blogg. It's a bit of a funny name, so I must admit that at first I smiled a bit. But then I read why the statue was there. Blogg was a lifeboat captain. He started out in lifeboats at the age of eighteen and served for fifty-three years. During that time, his boat went out 387 times and he rescued 873 lives. He won the Lifeboat Gold Medal for Gallantry three times, the Silver Medal four times, as well as the George Cross and the British Empire Medal. His record is unequalled in the lifeboat service. The statue says he was one of the bravest men that ever lived.

He looked pretty ordinary. His name was a bit odd, but he was a hero. 873 people lived because of him. How much more the call on our lives to rescue the lost and drowning?

Another time, I was up in Edinburgh on business. I took time out to go to the Royal Scots Dragoon Guards museum in the castle (it *was* free after all!). There are amazing stories there of bravery beyond the call of duty. One story is about a Private Dunsire. He climbed out of the trenches in 1914 and rescued a wounded soldier under very heavy gunfire. No sooner had he got back to safety, he heard another soldier cry out for help. Again he ran forward and again, under fire, he rescued the wounded soldier.

Another ordinary hero? I expect if he were alive today and being interviewed, he would say he was only doing his duty. We have a duty too. Paul says *'your task is to single-mindedly serve Christ'*.[24]

Walking, running, dreaming, rescuing. Whatever the picture we prefer, we are called to serve the one who died for us. It's the only way to live, the only way to colour the title page.

Across the finish line

I remember my first marathon race. It feels like I felt every emotion it was possible to feel in that race. Fear as I looked around at the start. Embarrassment as I compared my puny body to the fit young things around me. Exhilaration as we started. Doubt as I was overtaken by a 20 foot caterpillar (well, there were a number of soldiers inside it!). Sheer determination as I hit the 'wall' and kept going. And then there was the finish.

I had my name on my running vest, so as I ran up The Mall at the end of the race, people were calling out to me by name. I'd never seen them before, but there they were urging me on. It was an electrifying moment. After over 26 miles, my legs were about finished. I had no more energy. But the cries from the crowd spurred me on. I was running on sheer emotion, close to tears. 'Go on Ralph, you can do it!' came the cry. As the finishing line drew near I even managed to speed up a little. For me, it has remained one of the highlights of my life.

We read earlier, in Hebrews, that we have the crowds of history cheering us on. Men and women who have gone before us. The famous and the unknown. Everyone a hero, every one of them having finished the race. And so we finish with them. We cross the finishing line. We go from the title page into eternity. Our name is called. Our Lord greets us. The medal entitled, *'Well done good and faithful servant,'*[25] is placed around our neck. Immediately we take it off and place it at the feet of Jesus. What a day.

D.L. Moody put it rather well:

> 'Someday you will read in the papers that Moody is dead. Don't you believe a word of it. At that moment I shall be more alive than I am now. I was born of the flesh in 1837, I was born of the Spirit in 1855. That which is born of the flesh may die. That which is born of the Spirit shall live forever.'[26]

On that day we shall be more alive than ever. There will be no more tears, no more pain. Our bodies will be changed. As Tom Wright said, 'It's not that I'm a shadow of my former self, I'm a shadow of my future self'![27]

Only God knows the day

Whether Jesus comes first, or whether we die first, the day will come. But only God knows the day.

One of the tragedies of India is the prevalence of suicide, reflective of the Hindu lack of value on this life. But for all of us, it should be God and God alone that has the say on how long we each will live.

This was brought home to me with the atrocities of 9/11 when the two towers in New York collapsed as the planes hit them. I keep an email in my Bible from a US company I was dealing with at the time. Their office was in one of the towers. This is what the email says:

> 'I got your message requesting that I begin working on the pension plan ... As far as setting up a meeting with you in early September, how does September 11th in New York work for you?'

The email was dated 15th August 2001. I was supposed to be there – according to the email – on the day the towers were hit. I couldn't go. I'm still alive. (And I'm pleased to say, so is the lady at the company I was dealing with). Only God knows the day. Keeping that particular email in my Bible is a good reminder of this fact!

Dear reader...

Well, as Charlotte Bronte might have said, 'Dear reader, I've reached the end of this book.' The interesting thing about you

and me is that we may never meet. But I pray I have helped
put into you something of what God would have you to be.
My prayer for you:

> *'Keep your eyes on Jesus, who both began and finished this race we're*
> *in. Study how he did it. Because he never lost sight of where he was*
> *heading – that exhilarating finish in and with God.'*[28]

I trust you will run well and finish well. Always keep the hot-
line open, never forget the blood-line, keep looking down on
problems from heavenly places, take hold of God and let Him
take hold of you. May we all be captivated by the cry of
another country.

You are not alone on this journey. He has gone before, as
have many others. I'm running with you. You have friends all
around you. Right now you have approximately 2.1 billion
other Christians alive today and on your side. So don't give
up. Keep running. And should you hit the wall, listen to the
crowd calling you on.

In this chapter alone, we've sailed with lifeboat men, fought
with soldiers, and run the marathon. I want to return to the
sea for my final picture. More of a poem actually. As I leave
you to your ongoing God-life, my cry is the same as that of
Sir Francis Drake, who penned these words so long ago. Push
on in strength, courage, hope and love.

> 'Disturb us, Lord, when
> We are too well pleased with ourselves,
> When our dreams have come true
> Because we have dreamed too little,
> When we arrived safely
> Because we sailed too close to the shore.
>
> Disturb us, Lord, when
> With the abundance of things we possess

We have lost our thirst
For the waters of life;
Having fallen in love with life,
We have ceased to dream of eternity
And in our efforts to build a new earth,
We have allowed our vision
Of the new Heaven to dim.

Disturb us, Lord, to dare more boldly,
To venture on wider seas
Where storms will show your mastery;
Where losing sight of land,
We shall find the stars.
We ask You to push back
The horizons of our hopes;
And to push into the future
In strength, courage, hope, and love.'[29]

Notes

1. C.S. Lewis, *The Last Battle*, Bodley Head, 1956, ch. 16.
2. Psalm 139:15, AMP
3. Colossians 1:18, MSG
4. Luke 12:27–28
5. www.desiringgod.org
6. Romans 8:17; 1 Peter 4:12–19
7. 2 Corinthians 4:18, NLV
8. 1 Corinthians 13:12
9. Romans 12:1–2
10. Matthew 26:6–13
11. Philippians 2:9–11
12. Revelation 20:11–13; 2 Corinthians 5:10; Matthew 12:36
13. Matthew 25:31–46
14. Revelation 3:5; 20:12
15. Romans 8:12–14, MSG
16. Matthew 28:18–20
17. Acts 1:8
18. Hebrews 12:1
19. www.hyperhistory.net
20. Christian History Institute: http://chi.gospelcom.net

21. Hebrews 11:39–40, MSG
22. Hebrews 12:1–3, MSG
23. T.E. Lawrence (Lawrence of Arabia), *Seven Pillars of Wisdom*, 1922.
24. Romans 14:17, MSG
25. Matthew 25:21
26. John Pollock, *Moody without Sankey*, Hodder & Stoughton, 1983 reprint, p. 270.
27. Tom Wright lecture, Westminster Chapel, 12/03/08.
28. Hebrews 12:1, MSG
29. www.freshworship.org/node/248

About the Author

Ralph Turner is Director of Benefits for a large industrial company, and has also served on a number of Government and industry pensions and benefits groups.

Ralph is passionate about applying his faith to the everyday world – making the everyday special! He is a regular speaker both in the world of pensions and benefits and at Christian conferences.

As a teenager, Ralph heard God's call to work in India. He and his Indian wife, Rohini, use some of their holidays each year to work with churches in Andhra Pradesh in central India.

At KingsGate Community Church, Peterborough, Ralph has the privilege of working with a team of gifted people, resulting in a growing and exciting church. (www.kingsgateuk.com)

Ralph and Roh have four children. Nathan and Elspeth, the oldest, are both learning to apply their faith to their workplaces in Sheffield. Josh and Lois, the twins, are completing school back in Peterborough.

When not at work or serving in church life, Ralph likes to think he can keep fit and occasionally manages to go running with Wesley, his Chocolate Labrador. In his spare time he collects Indian stamps and watches *Doctor Who*.

More of Ralph

To read more of Ralph's thoughts and musings, go to www.mountain50.blogspot.com

We hope you enjoyed reading this New Wine book.
For details of other New Wine books
and a range of 2,000 titles from other
Word and Spirit publishers visit our website:
www.newwineministries.co.uk
email: newwine@xalt.co.uk